CAMBRIDGE LIBRARY COLLECTION

Books of enduring scholarly value

Cambridge

The city of Cambridge received its royal charter in 1201, having already been home to Britons, Romans and Anglo-Saxons for many centuries. Cambridge University was founded soon afterwards and celebrated its octocentenary in 2009. This series explores the history and influence of Cambridge as a centre of science, learning, and discovery, its contributions to national and global politics and culture, and its inevitable controversies and scandals.

Pembroke College Cambridge

This short history of Pembroke College, Cambridge appeared in 1936, during a particularly successful period for the college in terms of both academic and sporting achievements. Pembroke was founded in 1347, when Edward III granted Marie de St Pol, widow of the Earl of Pembroke, a licence for the foundation of a new educational establishment in the young University of Cambridge. The college flourished, and from the mid-nineteenth century expanded greatly. The author of this book, which is still regarded as the 'official history of Pembroke College', was a leading authority on the college's history. However, he died before the manuscript could be completed, and the final part was written as a postscript by S. C. Roberts, a former Master of the college. The book has delightful illustrations and a thorough index of the influential scholars, former students and benefactors connected with the college over the centuries.

T0384633

Cambridge University Press has long been a pioneer in the reissuing of out-of-print titles from its own backlist, producing digital reprints of books that are still sought after by scholars and students but could not be reprinted economically using traditional technology. The Cambridge Library Collection extends this activity to a wider range of books which are still of importance to researchers and professionals, either for the source material they contain, or as landmarks in the history of their academic discipline.

Drawing from the world-renowned collections in the Cambridge University Library, and guided by the advice of experts in each subject area, Cambridge University Press is using state-of-the-art scanning machines in its own Printing House to capture the content of each book selected for inclusion. The files are processed to give a consistently clear, crisp image, and the books finished to the high quality standard for which the Press is recognised around the world. The latest print-on-demand technology ensures that the books will remain available indefinitely, and that orders for single or multiple copies can quickly be supplied.

The Cambridge Library Collection will bring back to life books of enduring scholarly value (including out-of-copyright works originally issued by other publishers) across a wide range of disciplines in the humanities and social sciences and in science and technology.

Pembroke College Cambridge

A Short History

AUBREY ATTWATER
EDITED BY S.C. ROBERTS

CAMBRIDGE
UNIVERSITY PRESS

CAMBRIDGE UNIVERSITY PRESS

Cambridge, New York, Melbourne, Madrid, Cape Town, Singapore,
São Paolo, Delhi, Dubai, Tokyo

Published in the United States of America by Cambridge University Press, New York

www.cambridge.org
Information on this title: www.cambridge.org/9781108015332

© in this compilation Cambridge University Press 2010

This edition first published 1936
This digitally printed version 2010

ISBN 978-1-108-01533-2 Paperback

PEMBROKE COLLEGE
CAMBRIDGE:
A SHORT HISTORY

LONDON
Cambridge University Press
FETTER LANE

NEW YORK · TORONTO
BOMBAY · CALCUTTA · MADRAS
Macmillan

TOKYO
Maruzen Company Ltd

THE FOUNDRESS WITH S. CECILIA

(A page from her Breviary written in Paris, c. 1320)

PEMBROKE COLLEGE

CAMBRIDGE:

A Short History

BY

AUBREY ATTWATER

Edited with an Introduction and
a Postscript by
S. C. ROBERTS

CAMBRIDGE
AT THE UNIVERSITY PRESS
1936

CONTENTS

ILLUSTRATIONS

INTRODUCTION

MORE THAN ONE OF AUBREY ATTWATER'S FRIENDS regretted that he did not write a book; they consoled themselves, however, with the knowledge that he was with ever-growing enthusiasm preparing the material for what would have been a scholarly, humane and definitive history of the College that he most lovingly served. For several years before his death Aubrey had spent the greater part of his leisure in the study of College documents, and the more he studied them, the more deeply was he fascinated by them. From time to time he would display the first fruits of his labours in the form of a paper read to The Martlets on the Foundress or on Richard Crossinge, or on Gabriel Harvey, or on the history of the older College rooms. Such papers were, in fact, early drafts of chapters to be included in the *History* and provided clear evidence of the generous and scholarly scale on which the work was being planned. Or, again, he would contribute an essay on Pitt or on the College Plate or on the Servants or on the Buildings to the *Annual Gazette* of the College Society. Everyone who heard, or read, one of these papers rejoiced that the formidable task of writing a history of Pembroke was being faced in so gay a spirit. At the same time, some of us pleaded for some kind of preliminary sketch or outline which could suitably be given to members of the College as an introduction to the history of the foundation to which they belonged. Aubrey at first demurred. He was eager to devote all his energy and all his leisure to the heavy spade-work which the preparation of the *History* on the large scale demanded. Later, however, he concurred in the view that the drafting of the history in outline, say in 50 or 60 pages, would help him in his general survey of the material. To many of us this was a matter of great satisfaction, since we knew that if Aubrey set out to write an *Outline*, we should in fact get the *Short History* for which we had been pleading. By Easter 1935 this *Historiola*, as Aubrey liked to

call it, was in typescript up to the end of the eighteenth century
and the first portion of the final chapter had been drafted. In the
Long Vacation the work would have been completed.

Dis aliter visum. In July Aubrey died of the wound that he had
received in action more than twenty years before. In his will he
entrusted his manuscripts to me and it has been my clear, though
melancholy, duty to prepare the *Historiola* for publication. In
this task I have been greatly helped by the proof-reading of Mr
Whibley and Dr Minns, both of whom have made many valuable
corrections.

In the last chapter the illuminating sketch of the College as it
was in the period of Ainslie's Mastership (1828–1870) is Aubrey's.
His draft stopped at 1870 and the few pages which record some
of the salient features of College history from 1870 to the present
day are my own. They do not pretend to be anything more
than a postscript.

It remains to add that the *Historiola* represents but a fraction
of the knowledge of College history which Aubrey at the time
of his death had acquired, and was still acquiring. Many of his
notes, alas, are extremely difficult to decipher, but other parts of
his work had reached a stage of clearer codification. Much
valuable material awaits another enthusiast. *Utinam aliquis illius
viri optime de Collegio meriti aemulus inveniatur.*[1]

S. C. R.

[1] p. 75.

CHAPTER I

THE FOUNDATION OF THE COLLEGE

𝕸𝖆𝖗𝖞 𝖉𝖊 𝕾𝖙 𝕻𝖔𝖑, COUNTESS OF
PEMBROKE, BARONESS OF WEXFORD
IN IRELAND, AND OF MONTIGNAC,
BELLAC AND RANÇON IN FRANCE,
was the daughter of Guy, Count of St Pol in the Pas-de-Calais,
head of the younger branch of the great French house of Châtillon
of Châtillon-sur-Marne. During the Middle Ages this family
numbered among its great men Constables of France, Cardinals,
a Pope who was canonised and another Saint, St Charles of Blois,
a cousin of Mary de St Pol, and no family during the thirteenth
and fourteenth centuries married more often into the royal line
than the family of Châtillon. Their arms were *gules, three pales
vair with a chief or*, and this coat was said to have been granted to
a warrior of the family who was one of a party of Crusaders
surprised by the Turks when they had neither banners nor
blazons. They therefore cut up the scarlet cloaks lined with fur
which they were wearing, and displayed these strips instead of
banners and coats of arms. Having achieved victory they all
vowed that they would never display any heraldry in future other
than *gules* and *vair*. This legend is however discredited by André
Duchesne, the seventeenth-century historian of the Maison de
Chastillon. The father of Guy de St Pol had added to these arms,
"for difference", *a label of five points azure*. Guy de St Pol married
Mary of Brittany, who was the daughter of John de Dreux, Duke
of Brittany, and Beatrice daughter of King Henry III of England.
John de Dreux was great-grandson of Louis le Gros, King of
France. In the Foundress's veins therefore ran the blood of the
royal houses of both England and France.

On the ceiling of the College hall over the dais there are five
coats of arms. In the centre that of the Foundress; in the two

panels by the window those of England and France Ancient, in the other two panels are *checky or and azure a bordure gules for Dreux, a canton ermine for Brittany,* the arms of Mary of Brittany, the mother of the Foundress, and *azure a garb or,* which her father used on his secret seal, being the arms of Hugh Candavesne, an ancestor through whose daughter the county of St Pol came to the family of Châtillon.

Guy de St Pol died on April 6, 1317, leaving two sons and four daughters. The date of the birth of our Foundress is not known, but she must have been born between 1296 and 1303, so that she was about twenty when in 1321 she married Aymer de Valence, Earl of Pembroke. For this marriage the sanction of the Pope had to be obtained because Mary de St Pol was great-great-granddaughter of Isabel of Angoulême, who was grandmother of Aymer de Valence. Isabel of Angoulême was the wife of King John of England, and after his death she returned to her native Provence and married Hugh of Lusignan. This Hugh, involved in a quarrel with Saint Louis, King of France, lost his lands, and four of his children fled to England to the protection of their half-brother, Henry III. The eldest of these exiles, William de Valence, called so from his place of birth, became a great favourite of the king, who married him to Joan de Munchensy, granddaughter of William Marshall, Earl of Pembroke, one of the richest heiresses in England.

In return for these favours, William de Valence was a con-sistently loyal supporter of the king in his struggles against the barons under Simon de Montfort. His early life showed him an unscrupulous and rapacious partisan, but after the final defeat of Simon at Evesham he became a valuable and trusted servant both of Henry III and of his son, Edward I. Through the latter part of his life he was continually employed on tasks of difficulty and danger, in the Welsh marches, on the borders of Scotland and in France. In 1296, while on service in Gascony, he died, and he was buried in the abbey of Westminster. On the effigy on his tomb in the chapel of St Edmund the enamel on the shield which displays his arms is still preserved. To the Lusignan coat of *barry argent and azure* he had added, "for difference", *an orle of martlets gules.* Joan his wife survived him for some

SEAL OF AYMER DE VALENCE, EARL
OF PEMBROKE

SEAL OF THE COUNTESS OF PEMBROKE
(Arms of Valence and of Châtillon of St Pol)

years. She had shared his good and ill fortune, going into exile with him, defending his castles, smuggling gold out of the country to him, "by her woman's wit", as the chroniclers wrote, hidden in bales of wool. She had borne him three sons and four daughters. Daughters were to the medieval magnate more valuable investments than sons, and through his daughters William de Valence allied his family with the great influential families of Scotland, Wales, Ireland and Gascony. In her original statutes for the College the Foundress appointed the following days to be kept for the memory of her own and her husband's parents; for Guy de St Pol April 6, for Mary of Brittany May 5, for William de Valence June 23 and for Joan his wife September 9.

Aymer, the younger son of William de Valence, was named after an uncle, who, when probably illiterate and certainly too young, had been elected at King Henry's command Bishop of Winchester, and like him Aymer was originally intended for the Church. In May 1282 King Edward recommended him for preferment to the Pope as a youth of good ability by his study of letters, "since it was usual in England to provide the younger sons of magnates with a plurality of livings". But in July of this year his elder brother William was killed in a cavalry skirmish in Wales, and he became heir to his father. Even in the lifetime of his father he had been employed on the king's affairs, and on his succession to the lordship and vast estates of the Earls of Pembroke he began to take an important part in English life, being especially employed on diplomatic missions. The words in the College Commemoration of Benefactors describing him as "a person of the highest consideration in the reigns of Edward I and Edward II" are no exaggeration. Much of his service was on the Scottish borders against Wallace and Bruce, and Aymer's opposition to these two romantic national heroes of Scotland may account for the somewhat unfavourable estimate of him in many histories, but since Bruce murdered John Comyn, who was husband of Aymer's sister, some of his ruthless hostility was natural. He was one of the barons to whom Edward I on his death-bed committed the guidance of his frivolous son, Edward of Carnarvon, especially enjoining them not to let the prince's Gascon favourite, Piers Gaveston, return from banishment. Immediately on his accession

to the throne Edward II recalled Gaveston, and Aymer joined
with the other barons in opposition to the king. This hostility to
the king's favourite was attributed by the chroniclers partly to
Gaveston's success in tournaments over Aymer and his peers,
partly to his skill in inventing nicknames for them. Aymer,
because he was "tall and of a pallid countenance" he called Joseph
the Jew. But, when Gaveston was seized from the safe custody
of the Earl of Pembroke and murdered, Aymer, possibly because
he felt such an unknightly action a slur upon his honour, possibly
also moved by hereditary loyalty to his sovereign, left the baronial
party and became the chief and ablest adviser of King Edward.
He was with him at Bannockburn, and according to one account
led him away to safety when the battle was lost. Forming a
middle party between the barons under Lancaster and the king's
new favourites, the avaricious Despencers, he seems for some
years almost to have governed England. When he was at the
height of his power, his first wife died. She was Beatrice de
Clermont Néelles, daughter of a Constable of France, who in
1297 with Guy de St Pol had helped to negotiate a truce between
England and France at a conference at which Aymer had been
one of England's representatives. Soon after her death negotiations were opened for his marriage to Mary de St Pol. The kings
of both England and France petitioned the Pope for the necessary
sanction on the grounds that the match would help to preserve
peace between the two countries, and Edward may also have had
in mind the expediency of linking Aymer de Valence more closely
to himself through Mary de St Pol's uncle, John of Brittany, who
had lived in England all his life and was always of the king's party.

The marriage took place at Paris on July 5, 1321. At the church
door Aymer endowed his wife with two thousand pounds a year
of manorial lands, and she brought to him as her portion certain
lands in France and five hundred pounds a year from a grant made
to her father by the French king. On August 11, when Aymer
and his wife arrived in London, the barons rode out to meet them.
This was not, however, just a courtly ceremony to welcome to
England so distinguished a lady. During Aymer's brief absences
in France in the spring and summer of this year the baronial
opposition to the king and his favourite had flared into open

revolt. Enraged by the avarice of the Despencers, the barons, after consulting with the Earl of Lancaster, had come trooping up to London, and the city was almost in a state of siege. In a few days the king, supported by Aymer and by John of Brittany, seems to have effected a temporary settlement, but the turbulence which greeted our Foundress's arrival in her new country was to prove an omen of the troubled briefness of her married life. The reconciliation which had been effected soon broke down, Aymer's middle party dissolved, and for the next two years he seems to have been on service with the king, first in Kent, then in the marches of Wales, then against Lancaster, who was defeated at Borough Bridge and executed in the spring of 1322, and then against the Scots, who in the spring of 1322 in a raid into Yorkshire captured John of Brittany. At last, in the winter of 1323, Aymer appears to have been enjoying some peace in his East Anglian domains. But it was only for a while. Early in 1324 trouble was brewing in France, and in June he was sent over on an embassy. Partially successful, he was returning to England, when at Miville on the Seine, on June 23, he rose to take a turn in his chamber after dinner and fell speechless. In a few hours he was dead. His sudden death was attributed by some to God's anger at the part he had played against Lancaster and by others to the poison of Lancastrian exiles; apoplexy seems the more likely diagnosis. Through confusion with one of his successors to the earldom of Pembroke, who met his death in a tournament, a legend was afterwards established that he died at a tourney on the morning of his wedding day, and that our Foundress was "maid, wife and widow all in a day".

Aymer's body was brought to Westminster and buried in the beautiful tomb which still stands on the south side of the presbytery, near to the chantry which his widow endowed there for the repose of his soul.

Another legend still lives that our Foundress, shocked at the sudden death of her husband, turned at once to a life of pious devotion and charitable deeds, but for this too the evidence is not wholly convincing. For though from the date of his death her presence at Court can rarely be traced, and though it has been suggested that she may have become a tertiary in the order of

St Francis, yet it is twelve years from Aymer's death before we find any outstanding proof of her charitable endowments. At first she suffered at the hands of the young Despencer, and had to surrender the castles of Hereford and Haverfordwest and other property bequeathed to her by Aymer. Her dowry however remained safe, as well as her French lands and presumably her grant from the French treasury. Relations between England and France may have affected this part of her property, but when all Frenchmen in England were to be arrested, immunity was granted to her French servants and retainers, including one Mabel du Bois, for whom her statutes for Pembroke College were later to prescribe the prayers of her scholars, because she had been in her service for "about fifty years". On the deposition of Edward II she fared scarcely better, and her marriage was actually granted to Queen Isabel's lover, Roger Mortimer. She escaped this peril, and almost immediately after the young king, Edward III, had seized the reins of government into his own hands, she went over to France "on the king's business", escorted by knights and clerks who had been in the service of Aymer de Valence. Her marriage had been arranged as a pledge of peace between the kings of England and France; this journey to France at a moment when Edward III seems to have been aiming at peace with France may also have had a diplomatic object. She remained in France for more than two years, during which she was busy from time to time about an exchange of some of her French lands for English land belonging to her uncle John of Brittany, now resident in France. But his illness and death seem to have prevented this exchange. On her return to England King Edward appointed her guardian of his infant daughter Joan, and rewarded her for her services with certain lands in Kent and at Denny near Cambridge. It was however when the war between England and France had become inevitable through Edward's claim to the French throne, that the record of her two great charitable foundations begins. In 1336 she gave lands to the convent of Minoresses at Waterbeach, and in 1339 she obtained leave to found a new abbey for them at Denny. Other charitable schemes that she seemed to be considering were a chantry at Westminster, a college of secular canons and a Carthusian monastery, and it is not til

1346 that we have any evidence that the College entered into her plans. A Franciscan apologist, writing some fifty years later, claimed that as Lady Balliol had been persuaded by her Franciscan Confessor to found a college at Oxford, so Mary de St Pol in founding a college at Cambridge and another in Paris was following the advice of a Confessor of the same order. In 1341 a Franciscan friar, John Peverel, held that office in the household of Mary de St Pol, and it may have been on his advice that she acted. When on September 14, 1346, our Foundress acquired property in Cambridge itself, we can assume that her mind was made up, and on December 24, 1347, at Guildford, on the eve of the Christmas festivities at which with masques and shows Edward III was about to celebrate his capture of Calais and also the betrothal of Princess Joan to Don Pedro of Spain, he signed the charter of our foundation.

In 1347 there were only four colleges in Cambridge, Peterhouse and Clare, founded in 1284 and 1326, and Michael House (1326) and King's Hall (1337), which were both later to be absorbed into Trinity College. Most of the students in the University lived in lodgings or in hostels. The great advantages of the endowed college were obvious, and between 1347 and 1352 four more came into being, Pembroke (1347), Gonville Hall (1348), Trinity Hall (1350) and Corpus Christi (1352). Edward III's charter gave power to our Foundress to found a house of scholars in Cambridge and to establish in it a Keeper and thirty scholars or more according to her wish, living under a fixed rule and studying in the various faculties in the University according to her statutes, and to give them property in Cambridge for their habitation, and to endow them with advowsons of churches up to a hundred pounds. In her first deed of gift to her scholars the Foundress states that she makes the gift for the salvation of her soul, and of the souls of Aymer de Valence, Guy de St Pol and Mary of Brittany.

The first property was the "great messuage of Hervey de Stanton", which she had bought in 1346, and it consisted of a house and yards at the corner of what are now Pembroke Street and Trumpington Street; in 1351 she added the property next adjacent to the south, called University Hostel. In 1363 she purchased for the College, as a garden, a strip of meadow between walls lying behind these two properties, to which the College added a further strip in 1404; these two strips have been preserved as a garden ever since, and are now occupied by the bowling green and orchards in the Fellows' garden.

According to the custom of other colleges the Foundress had intended her scholars to worship in the parish church of St Botolph, and she took some steps towards acquiring for them the advowson of that church, but in 1355 and 1366 she obtained papal bulls to allow them to have their own chapel, the first college chapel to be built in Cambridge. She must first have lodged her scholars in the houses existing on the site, but by 1357 there is evidence that building had begun, and probably the first court of the College was completed in her lifetime, a small enclosed court about half the size of the present Old Court, with the chapel where now is the old library, and kitchen and hall roughly on their present site.

The Foundress endowed her College in the usual manner of the time by appropriating to her scholars, as the king's charter allowed her, the advowsons of the churches of Saxthorpe and of Tilney in Norfolk, and of Waresley in Huntingdonshire. This method of endowment was in effect to assign the tithe to the religious or learned foundation, subject to the condition that the foundation appointed a vicar, provided him with a vicarage and assigned to him an adequate portion of the tithe. The details of these appropriations had to be settled to the satisfaction of the bishop of the diocese, and the whole business was, for our Foundress, complicated by irregularities in the purchase of Tilney, to which, while negotiations were in progress, the king presented a young clerk of his own household, so that in actual fact the College did not come into its full share of Tilney until the early years of the next century. The manor and advowson of Saxthorpe had formed part of the Foundress's dowry, but she had converted to fee-simple a life interest in the advowson; Tilney and Waresley she had purchased. She also gave to the College two rents which she had bought from her uncle John of Brittany, one at Whissendene in Rutlandshire, and the other at Repton, which the College a few years later exchanged for a rent out of lands belonging to Repton

Priory at Gransden in Huntingdonshire. The total of the three advowsons was £106. 13s. 4d. and of the two rents £14.

The problem of the early statutes of the College remains unsolved. In the College Treasury are two documents, each of which purports to be the statutes given by the Foundress to her College in 1347, yet they embody two codes which are materially different, and it is obvious that one represents an earlier stage in the making of the statutes. Yet both documents, since they refer to the Foundress as of "illustrious memory", were presumably written after her death. Of the code which is obviously the later, there is a copy in the University Registry, but since this is bound in a parchment sheet upon which are recorded the receiver's accounts for the Foundress's manor of St Florence in Pembrokeshire some time during her lifetime, and since the College never had anything to do with this manor, it seems likely that this copy was made by some clerk of her household. It is always claimed for William de Merton that by the statutes which he made for his College at Oxford he invented the true type of the English college, an endowed and self-governing body subject only to limited interference by an external Visitor, while at the University of Paris the colleges were usually put under control of external "Rectors" or "Proctors". Lady Balliol had preserved the Parisian type of college in her statutes for her College at Oxford, when she set over the Master and Fellows two Proctors, one of whom seems always to have been a Franciscan friar. The earlier of the two codes of our statutes prescribes two "Rectors" with certain powers over the College, one of whom had to be a Franciscan. In the later code all traces of these Rectors have been removed, and their powers delegated to the Master or to the Society as a whole. In 1357 one Rayner d'Ambonnay and Robert de Stanton, a Franciscan friar, went out to Avignon to expedite at the papal court the business of the appropriations, "in which service", as Fuller relates, "(well forwarded but not finished) they there ended their lives, and in gratitude to their memory a Statute was made in the College that their obsequies should yearly be kept in the month of July". It is possible that d'Ambonnay and Friar Robert de Stanton were the first Rectors.

In 1362, however, there are some signs that the College was

assuming more control of its affairs, and possibly about this time
the Foundress, devoted though she was to the Franciscan order,
may have been advised of its unpopularity in the University, and
released her College from its supervision. In the second code,
however, she added an emphatic affirmation of her own powers
in the affairs of her College. In both codes it is laid down that
the power of interpreting statutes is to remain with her in her lifetime, "quia cuius est condere, eius est etiam interpretari", but in
the later code she added a clause giving herself power to nominate
or remove Fellows. In both codes the name of the College is
ordered to be for ever "the hall or house of Valence-Marie", a
name which beautifully perpetuated the joint memory of Aymer
de Valence and herself, but in Cambridge even before her death
the "House of Valence-Marie" was "vulgariter" named "Pembroke Hall". The College was founded "in augmentum cleri et
studii", and of the thirty *scholares* twenty-four were to be *majores*,
or what are now called Fellows, and six *minores*, or what are now
called Scholars, "grammatici vel sophistae", boys studying
grammar, who as soon as they reached the standing of bachelors
were eligible, if fitted, for election as Fellows. These *scholares
minores* are to be chosen as far as possible from those parishes of
which the College holds the advowson. The chief study of the
scholares majores is to be theology, although one of them may study
medicine, and one other for a short time may, though only as
a help to the study of theology, study law. A Frenchman at
Cambridge or Oxford is to have preference in the election of
Fellows, and not more than a quarter of the whole number of
the Fellows may come from the same county. The earlier of the
two codes contains a provision for a Librarian, in the later the
books are to be under the care of the Treasurer. The earlier code
prescribes a manciple ("A man loyal and honest, careful and
prudent in all that concerns provisions"), a cook, a barber and
a laundress, the later code generally orders "all useful servants
with a barber and laundress". Both codes contain an injunction
to the Master or Keeper and Fellows to be well-wishing and
favourable to all monks and especially to Franciscan friars, to give
all counsel and aid within their knowledge and power to the
sisters of Denny Abbey, as being sprung from the same root and

stem, or as the historian Fuller wrote: "She enjoyned also her Fellows of *Pembroke Hall*, to visit those Nuns, and give them ghostly counsel on just occasions; who may be presumed (having not only a fair invitation, but full injunction) that they were not wanting both in their courteous and conscientious addresses unto them."

For the affairs of her College were not the only cares of Mary de St Pol during the last years of her life. At Denny Abbey she experienced great trouble with certain recalcitrant nuns who refused to leave the old convent at Waterbeach till she caused them to be swiftly removed to their new quarters. In the year after the foundation of the College the Black Death reached East Anglia, and it is possible that loss of her clerks and the general disturbed state of the country which ensued may have hindered progress. In 1353, however, she must have felt that the House of Valence Marie and Denny Abbey could stand without her immediate supervision, and she set out for France to redeem certain debts owing to her. She appears also to have formed in the same year a plan for founding some sort of college or places in a college in the University of Paris, and in June 1356, out of the debts owing to her by the King of France, arrears presumably of her marriage portion, she founded a college in Paris, of which she appointed Rayner d'Ambonnay Master. But as the Black Prince was already making his great raid across France and on September 14 at Poitiers the French king became his prisoner, the French king's debts to Mary de St Pol were not likely to be paid and her college at Paris got no further than an intention, a monument of which is perhaps to be found in the Pembroke Treasury in a list of debts between Guy de St Pol and the French Crown. Rayner d'Ambonnay came back with the Foundress to England and she consoled him with the rectory of St Florence in Pembrokeshire which formed part of the dowry settled on her after Aymer's death, and employed him in the affairs of her College. At this juncture there is some evidence that she, in concert with the Queen-mother Isabel, took part in endeavouring to effect peace between England and France. But when war was resumed, in 1372, the country of her birth disowned her and another did homage for her lands there. Yet in her will she left gifts to the Queen of France, and to the king a sword without a point to be carried to him by her chamberlain, "mon bien aimé Willecok", who was also an executor of her will.

During the later years of her life she seems to have been much at Denny. Her other residences were at Fotheringay, Anstey, Cheshunt and Great Braxted, and as her will was made at Braxted on February 20, 1377, with a codicil dated March 13 at the same place, it may be presumed that it was at Braxted that she died on March 16 of that year. She directed that her body should be buried without great cost in the habit of a Minoress in the choir of Denny Abbey, where her tomb had already been made between the choirs of the nuns and the seculars. This abbey, now a farmhouse, the College purchased in 1929, but the ravages of five centuries have obliterated all trace of the Foundress's tomb.

There is no picture of Mary de St Pol. The portrait in the College hall is based on an eighteenth-century fiction, and the representation of her in her breviary preserved in the University Library and upon her own seal and the seal of her College are probably conventional and at any rate too small to give any idea of her likeness.

CHAPTER II

THE MEDIEVAL COLLEGE

The first sixty years of the history of the College provide but a scanty record. Though the royal charter allowed thirty or more scholars, of whom twenty-four were to be Fellows and six Scholars, tradition records that the Foundress herself only provided for six Fellows and two Scholars. Down to the year 1400 less than forty names of members of the College can be traced, and most of these are but names. Even the succession of the Masters is uncertain. In 1354 Robert de Thorpe is named as Master in a receipt for "first fruits" paid for Saxthorpe to the Pope's collector. He was certainly not the famous Chief Justice and Lord Chancellor under Edward III, often wrongly called the first Master of Pembroke. In the fourteenth century a man's place of birth often did duty for his surname, and there are many places called Thorpe in England. Our Robert de Thorpe was probably a Suffolk man, who had held a living in the gift of our Foundress, and had played some part in the endowment of Denny Abbey. In 1363 or 1364 he resigned the Mastership of the College and was succeeded by Thomas de Bingham, who had been Proctor of the University in 1363. The change may mark a certain step in the independence of the College, for among the College deeds is a note that the papal bull for the foundation of the College, hitherto kept by the Foundress, "en la garde madame", was on November 25, 1365, handed over in London to "Maistre Thomas". Bingham seems to have been an energetic and capable man, and was very active in the tangled transactions over the advowsons. He was still Master in 1373, but in 1374 he resigned a living which he held by the gift of the Foundress, and probably went to reside at Wells as sub-dean. Probably at about the same time he ceased to be Master, and was succeeded by John Tinmew or Tynmouth. Tinmew had been a Fellow of the College, and prominent in its affairs as well as in those of the University. He was the "Maistre John Timmie" whom the Foundress appointed an executor of her will. Books which he gave to the College are still in the College library. He died in 1385 and Richard Morys is first mentioned as Master in 1389. Of him nothing is known beyond his name, which last appears in the College records in 1401. In 1392 he was witness of a gift of land to Denny Abbey, thus showing himself obedient to the Foundress's valedictory statute which bade her scholars to be active and helpful in the affairs of the sister foundation.

Of the earliest Fellows of the College our knowledge is still scantier. A name such as Thomas Waresley, Proctor in 1388, shows compliance with the statute giving preference in elections to those coming from the parishes of which the College held the advowson. John Lavenham, a monk of Colchester, represents a type of scholar common at the Universities at this time. Pembroke has no claim to Michael Cawston, Master of Michael-house and Chancellor of the University; the Pembroke Cawston is clearly a younger man. The memory of a few of the earliest Fellows is preserved by the record of their gifts of books to the College library, and some of their gifts are still there. Among these benefactors was one William of Bottisham, who must have been a Fellow while the Foundress was still alive and is the first on the long roll of bishops bred in the College. A Dominican friar, he won the favour of Richard II by his preaching, and was given by him the title of Bishop of Bethlehem, then promoted to Llandaff in 1386 and in 1389 to Rochester. The first of the Pembroke poets also makes his appearance before the death of the Foundress. James son of Nicholas from Denmark wrote and illuminated in 1363 a long poem which is now in the British Museum. The book consists of a series of elaborately illuminated pattern-poems on Death, followed by a long panegyric of Aymer de Valence, in the course of which he praises also the Foundress, whose scholar he was, as

> Mater egenorum, pia tutrix inferiorum,
> Religiosorum fundatrix clericulorum.

and to her charity he calls upon Cambridge and Denny to bear witness.

One other fourteenth-century Fellow was regarded as a

sufficiently important benefactor for his name to be inserted in the statutes. Thomas More appears to have been a clerk in the household of Richard II's Queen Anne, and his long list of preferments starts in 1389 and ends in 1406 with the deanery of St Paul's. He died in 1421, and was a benefactor also to the University and to the Queen's College, Oxford.

During the first sixty years of the College some increase was made to its site and to its endowments. The Foundress had in 1349 bought a farm at Burwell and in 1369 she had conveyed it to trustees, who held it for the College. One of those trustees, Arnold de Pynkney, an executor of her will, was trustee also for the strip of garden, and in 1381, on that Sunday when the Peasants' Revolt had spread to Cambridge and there was riot and looting, he conveyed this garden and the farm at Burwell to certain Fellows of the College, and if the document can be trusted, this transaction was witnessed by the very magnates whose houses the mob had been that day attacking. When Parliament met in 1389 at Cambridge the College obtained the necessary licence in mortmain to hold the strip of garden and also to acquire one further property to the south of the College along Trumpington Street, a tenement known as Cosyn's Place, which lay along a line drawn across the present Old Court and under the south range of buildings in Ivy Court. This strip of land they also converted into a garden. Later still they obtained the necessary licence for the farm at Burwell and for the southern strip of the main garden, which they had purchased in 1401.

After Richard Morys John Sudbury appears as Master in 1406, and from 1412 slightly more detailed information about the College based upon the accounts is available. For another hundred and fifty years this information is limited to extracts made in the seventeenth century by Matthew Wren from "2 olde account bookes in folio", which have been missing ever since. From the accounts of commons Wren notes that in 1412 there were "but 9 fellows et unus puer". His extracts from these old accounts not only give the names of Fellows, but also of others living in the College, and paying for their rooms that "pensio pro camera", which is the origin of the title "pensioner" still applied to undergraduates who are not scholars on the foundation. These pensioners however of the fifteenth century were mostly more elderly men, ex-Fellows who stayed on in College after either preferment or a choice of law as a study had rendered them ineligible to retain their Fellowships, or beneficed clergymen perhaps on leave from their parishes to study theology, but more likely seeking through the study of canon law to make themselves fit for office in some great household. In 1412 there is among the pensioners an unnamed Rector of Calais, and in 1413 Reginald, son of Lord Grey, pays for a room. He may have been a younger son of that Lord Grey of Ruthin who in 1410 had after a long suit won his claim to bear the arms of John Hastings, who had married the sister of Aymer de Valence. From 1419 to 1433 one Thomas Lavenham, a writer on theology, and a former Fellow, lived in College, but it is possible that he had some claim to the gratitude of the Society for his help in acquiring one more property to the south of the College along Trumpington Street. This property, known as Bolton's or Knapton's Place, was separated from Cosyn's Place by a piece of land belonging to a chantry in the Church of Little St Mary,[1] and it does not seem to have been adapted to College purposes. John Sudbury is recorded as the benefactor responsible for this addition to the College site, and though he resigned the Mastership in 1430 he continued to live in College till his death in 1435, when he bequeathed to the College a number of books, of which one [MS. 120 *Ezekiel Glossatus*] is among the most valuable treasures of the College library, being the earliest stamped binding to be found in Cambridge.

Under Sudbury's Mastership three Fellows were elected to whom the College owed the still greater growth of position which was imminent. William Lyndewode, a Lincolnshire man, had been a pensioner at Gonville Hall, and was elected to a Fellowship at Pembroke in 1407. In ecclesiastical and diplomatic affairs he became one of the leading ministers of Henry VI, and he was from 1423 to 1446 Keeper of the Privy Seal. In 1442 he was appointed Bishop of St David's. Yet for all his busy employment in Church and State he found time to compile his *Provinciale*, the most important collection on English canon law to this day.

[1] This piece of land was conveyed to the College in 1549.

LOWER COVER OF BINDING OF EZEKIEL GLOSSATUS,
c. 1190

During his lifetime he gave to the College ten pounds, to which Mr Robert Pyke, Fellow 1425–36, added another five, to form a "chest", which soon became known as "Lyndewode and Pyke's chest". The old statute of this chest states that one of the first among acts of charity is to relieve scholars of the distracting troubles of poverty so that more fruitfully, because more freely, they may reap the harvest of virtue and science in the field of academic exercise, and the fund was first used to provide money which Fellows might need and could obtain by pledging or pawning a book to the chest. One book so deposited by John of Lowestoft in 1454 and forfeited by default is still in the College library. Later in the eighteenth century, when the fund had been increased to a hundred pounds by Bishop Wren, it became a working cash balance for the Bursar to enable him to buy provisions at favourable prices. By the statutes of 1926 it was restored to something nearer its original purpose as a fund for grants in aid in sickness or in supplement to pensions for the College staff.

John Somerset, who was a Fellow in 1410, was twice Proctor, and also studied medicine in Paris. He was physician and tutor to Henry VI and from 1441 to 1446 Chancellor of the Exchequer. He lost his offices in 1451, and seems to have fallen into some poverty, dying in 1455. In the College library is a manuscript (MS. 137) of the medical writings of Avicenna given by Somerset with an autograph inscription,

benedicta igitur sit aula illa nobilis, qua educatus sum, et eius fundatrix devotissima domina Maria de Sancto Paulo.

John Langton, of the Lincolnshire and not the Cumberland family of that name, was elected a Fellow in 1412, and was a chaplain to Henry V's Queen Katherine, and afterwards to Henry VI.

These three men from their position at Court were able to win for Pembroke the favour of Henry VI before he began to spend all his thought and exchequer on Eton and King's College. When Sudbury resigned the Mastership in 1428, Langton was elected his successor, and in 1439 and 1440 the king gave to the College the priory of Lynton with the chapel of Isleham,[1] and the manor

[1] The chapel at Isleham, after being long used as a barn, has now been scheduled as an Ancient Monument.

and advowson of Soham, which had been confiscated during the wars of his father's reign from the alien monasteries of St Jacutus de Insula in Brittany and of the Virgin Mary of Pyne in Poitou. This was a very substantial addition to the endowments of the College. In his deed of gift the king speaks of the great number of scholars of the College, who in their application to theology and other branches of learning "ferventissimo studio desudassent desudareque in laudem Dei in dies non desistant", and the Society in a letter of thanks says that his pity had raised the College from the misfortunes into which it had been cast down to a sufficiency which it is scarcely believed to have enjoyed since its foundation. Fuller the historian comments on King Henry's benefactions:

King Henry the Sixth was so great a favourer of this House, that it was termed his *adopted Daughter* (King's Coll. onely, being accounted his *natural sonne*) and great were his benefactions bestowed thereon. But above all we take notice of that passage in his Charter *granting* (repeated in another of *King Edward's* confirming) lands to this House

Notabile & insigne, & quam pretiosum Collegium, quod inter omnia loca Universitatis (prout certitudinaliter infor- mamur) mirabiliter splendet & semper resplenduit.

Now although it is frequent for *inferiors* to flatter their *superiors*, it is seldom seene, that *Subjects* are praised by their *Soveraigns* without due cause, as this doth appear true to such as seriously peruse our foregoing Catalogue. And though the commendation in the King's *Charta*, be confined to Cambridge; yet it may be extended to any College in Christendom of the same proportion, for Students therein. I say (as the Apostele in another kinde) *that there may be equality*, let *Pembroke Hall* be compared with any foundation in Europe, not exceeding it in bigness time, and number of Members, and it will acquit itself not conquered in all learned and liberal capacities.

King Henry VI thus came to be regarded as the second Founder of the College, and in 1440 the Society spent twenty-six shillings and sixpence on pictures of his arms and those of the Foundress. The statutes prescribed that the Foundress should be celebrated four times a year at the Feasts of St Leonard (November 6), St Vincent (January 23), St John ante Portam Latinam (May 6) and St Kenelm (July 17); in 1448 the College decreed a similar honour to King Henry at the Feasts of St Fabian and St Sebastian (January 20), St "Tedde" (March 18), St Medward and St Gildard (June 8), and St Kenneth (October 11).

It was Langton who persuaded Henry to found King's College, and in 1441 he, as Chancellor of the University, with Lyndewode as Keeper of the Privy Seal and Somerset as Chancellor of the Exchequer were members of the first commission instructed to make statutes for that great foundation. Langton was also much concerned with the business of its buildings and endowments. This preoccupation of the Master was felt by the Fellows of Pembroke, and having planned to add to their own buildings by the construction of a new library over the hall, they were forced to solicit the king's favour through other channels, which they did in a letter probably to Somerset, suggesting that a gift of trees from the royal forests would be very welcome. In 1447 Langton reaped the reward of his services to the king in his appointment to the see of St David's, but fifteen days after his consecration (in the unfinished chapel of King's College, of which he has been held to be the architect) he died.

The nineteen years of his Mastership had seen great expansion in the College. There had been the benefactions of the king; a new library had been begun and the chapel completed by the erection of the bell tower expressly sanctioned in the papal bull of 1366. And the College was still feeling its way southward along the King's highway to Trumpington. South of Bolton's Place was a property belonging to St John's Hospital, upon which stood a hostel for students known as St Thomas's Hostel. After some litigation the College in 1446 established a right to appoint an Exterior Principal to this hostel, while the students continued to elect the Interior Principal, and the hostel seems to have soon become a kind of annexe to the College in which the Fellows of the College taught and the students of which paid fees to the College. Such an attachment naturally added to the reputation of the College besides increasing its income. In 1448 Queen Margaret petitioned her husband to be allowed to assume the

2-2

patronage of a new foundation, which was to become Queens'
College,

to laud and honneure of sexe femenine, like as two noble and
devoute contesses of Pembroke and of Clare founded two collages
in the same universite called Pembroke hall and Clare hall, the
wiche are of grete reputacon for good and worshipful clerkis,
that by grete multitude have be bredde and brought forth in
them.

In the great multitude of good and worshipful clerks bred in
Pembroke Hall [1] the queen would doubtless have put first such
men as Lyndewode, Somerset and Langton. But other Pembroke
clerks had become famous. William Booth, of a powerful
Lancashire family, had started life as a student of law at Gray's
Inn, but afterwards came to Pembroke, probably as a pensioner
since he was apparently never a Fellow. In 1447 he had been
appointed to the bishopric of Coventry and Lichfield, and he
became in 1452 Archbishop of York. Of his half-brother
Laurence, Bishop of Durham in 1457 and Archbishop of York
in 1476, more must be said later. John Marshall, a Fellow in 1444,
though he appears to have pawned to a bookseller Somerset's
gift to the library without the permission of the College at a cost
to them of £1. 6s. 4d., became in 1478 Bishop of Llandaff.
Edward Story, Fellow in 1444, became Master of Michaelhouse
in 1450, Bishop of Carlisle in 1468, and of Chichester in 1478.
He built the beautiful cross in the market square at Chichester,
and was a considerable benefactor of the College. Another clerk,
a famous preacher of the time, Thomas Westhaugh, became Prior
of Syon Monastery and gave about twenty books to the College
library. Some of the pensioners also gave books to the library,
as Thomas Anlaby of a wealthy Yorkshire family and Peter Irford,
who had in his youth been a follower of Wycliffe's opinions, but
having recanted became a prominent person in the University
and ended by being a member of the Royal Commission which
examined the heresies of Reginald Pecock. He had also been

[1] Among them no less than four were made commissioners to draw
up the statutes for the new "queens' college", i.e. William Booth, John
Somerset, Hugh Damlet and Peter Hirford.

Confessor to the Duke of Bedford and was an early Fellow of Queens' College.

Growth, however, of wealth and position[1] brought responsibilities and anxiety. Under the weak government of Henry VI and his ministers disorder was rife, and the College felt the need and value of a Master of Langton's capacity and Court influence. But the statutes prescribed that the Master should be elected from among the Fellows, and so on Langton's death they elected Hugh Damlet. He had been Proctor, and was therefore presumably a man of affairs. The books which he gave to the library are proof of his learning, and the part he played in the prosecution of Pecock shows that he was regarded as a theologian. But he had apparently little influence at Court, and in 1450 the College petitioned the Pope for dispensation from the statute compelling them to elect a Master from their own body. A bull of Pope Nicholas V granted their petition on the grounds that the Fellows were bound to be poor men, having only small benefices or none at all, and consequently unable to resist the malignities of men, whereby many disadvantages were likely to befall the College. The bull is dated November 1450, but before the end of April Hugh Damlet had already resigned the Mastership and retired to a living in London and the Fellows had anticipated the granting of the dispensation by electing Laurence Booth to succeed him.

Booth was illegitimate, but he had some time before received papal dispensation of any disabilities thereby involved, and by 1450 by his own undoubted ability and the influence of his family he had his foot well up the ladder of ecclesiastical preferment. Since in 1452 he became Chancellor to Queen Margaret, we may presume that his apprenticeship in the public service had been served in her household, where his half-brother William had held high office, and this would strengthen the attachment of the College to the Lancastrian cause. His election was quickly justified. In 1451 he obtained for the College the perpetual lease from St John's Hospital of St Thomas's Hostel, at a yearly rent of

[1] In the accounts of Peterhouse, 1447, there is a note that the Lord Beaumont, then Constable of England and perhaps on his way to the Parliament at Bury, spent the night in Pembroke.

six shillings and eightpence, a rent which Pembroke College still pays to St John's College. The students of the Hostel became therefore still more closely attached to the College, and in 1457 there were thirty-four there, each paying a "pensio" of eightpence a term to the College. Booth also carried to completion the new library over the hall, and apparently either paid for it himself or obtained a sufficient benefaction to relieve the College of the burden of its cost. In 1456 he became Dean of St Paul's and in the next year Bishop of Durham. As Chancellor of the University he set in hand the building of new Schools for the public acts and lectures. His promotion naturally entailed long absences from College, but involved as he was in the fortunes of the house of Lancaster the Yorkist victory of 1461 brought to an end for a while his public service. In 1462 he was suspended from his bishopric, and though it was restored to him two years later, he was given leave to absent himself from parliaments and to live where he wished. Matthew Wren found evidence in the accounts of commons that from 1462 to 1466 he was in residence in College for long periods. The triumph of the White Rose might have meant resumption by the Crown of the gifts made to the College by Henry VI, but through the intervention of George Neville, Bishop of Exeter, and his brother the great Earl of Warwick, these benefactions were confirmed by Edward IV. This intervention has been attributed to the fact that a niece of Booth had married a Neville, the Earl of Westmorland, but this was a Lancastrian branch of the Neville family and generally at odds with the rest of the clan. During these years of enforced retreat in his own College Booth did much for its estates and buildings. He acquired the whole site of another hostel lying between the College and St Botolph's Church. St Thomas's Hostel provided a profitable lodging house for paying pupils; the chief advantage of St Botolph's Hostel appears to have been that it had useful offices such as a bakery and a brewery. In 1462 the tower that was to give access to the new library and it may be also to the Master's chambers was built and a rood-loft added to the chapel. In 1473 Booth was back in favour, and was made Keeper of the Great Seal, and in 1476 he became Archbishop of York, and the same year the College gates were painted, possibly in honour of so great an event. On his death in 1480 he bequeathed to the College the manor and advowson of Orton Waterville near Peterborough. Bishop Andrewes used to name Booth Pembroke's "third Founder", and he deserves the title through the way in which his benefactions had extended and enriched the College.

Under him the fame of the College as a nursery of great and worshipful clerks was increased. Thomas Langton, Fellow in 1461, was Bishop successively of St David's, Salisbury, and Winchester, and Provost of the Queen's College, Oxford, and he was elected Archbishop of Canterbury in 1501, but died before his consecration. John Blythe, a pensioner in 1478, while he was Archdeacon of Stow, having taken his degree of bachelor only the year before, was Bishop of Salisbury in 1494 and Master of the Rolls. Richard Stubbs, Fellow in 1467, became Master of Clare Hall, and William Chubbes, Fellow in 1466, was the first Master of Jesus College. It has also been held, though on no real evidence, that John Alcock, the Founder of Jesus College, was at Pembroke. Another Fellow under Booth was Richard Sokburn, who probably gave the cup which is now called the Foundress's cup. William Atkinson, an original Fellow of Jesus College, translated the *Imitatio Christi*, and procured benefactions in land for the College. William Rawson, Master of Jesus College, at Rotherham, gave books to the College library. Gerard Skipwith seems to have been a particularly active Fellow for over fifty years, writing books in the College library and managing the affairs of the College as Booth's deputy. He and his brother Nicholas were also considerable benefactors. Another Fellow was Humphry Fitzwilliam, who was Vice-Chancellor in 1501. Among the pensioners, too, the name of L'Estrange shows the reputation which the College must have had. Booth's personal influence in drawing to Pembroke these alumni may perhaps be seen in the large proportion of men from the north country. Langton and Rawson were from Westmorland, Blythe from Derbyshire, Fitzwilliam from Cheshire, Chubbes, the Skipwiths, Atkinson and Sokburn were all Yorkshiremen. Out of sixty-eight names of Fellows and pensioners recorded between 1450 and 1500 only forty-one can be traced to their place of birth, and of these twenty-eight were north-country men.

For ten years before Booth's death Thomas Scot, generally known as Thomas Rotherham, from his place of birth, had been the most princely benefactor of the Universities and of learning generally. An early Fellow of King's College, he had been Keeper of the Privy Seal in 1467 and Bishop of Rochester in 1468 and of Lincoln in 1472; by 1480 he had been already five times Chancellor of Cambridge University, and had carried on the work on the Schools, which Booth had inaugurated, by adding a library, to which he himself gave over two hundred books.[1] During these years his benefactions to Lincoln College, Oxford, had earned him the title of second Founder of that College. John Blythe, who had been a pensioner at Pembroke in 1478, was his nephew, and in 1480, when Booth died, the Fellows elected Rotherham Master. A few months later he also succeeded Booth as Archbishop of York.

By this election, however, the Fellows did not reap the benefactions which they appear to have expected, and they began to experience some of the disadvantages of electing a great magnate. Booth had been often absent; Wren notes that under Rotherham Chubbes is the first to be named President. The statutes allowed the Master a "locum tenens", but the dignified title of President, still preserved in the College lists as "Mr Praeses", suggests that during these years more responsibility began to devolve upon the Master's deputy. Rotherham was much preoccupied at this time with the foundation of his College of Jesus in his native town. Moreover, in 1483 by his support of the young King Edward V and of the Queen-Mother he lost the favour of Richard Duke of Gloucester, and was imprisoned. The University petitioned for clemency, "we must nedes mourne and sorowe, desolate of comfurth, unto we hear and understande youre benynge Spyrite of Pite to hymwarde, which is a grete Prelate in the Realme of England". He was soon released from prison, but his career as a statesman was practically finished. In 1488 he resigned the Mastership of the College, and when he died in 1500 neither King's College, of which he had been a Fellow, nor Pembroke,

[1] Richard Cockeram, of Pembroke, while Proctor, compiled a catalogue of these books.

of which he had been Master, found a mention among the many charitable bequests in his will.

On his resignation the Fellows continued the policy of electing into the Mastership one who by his position could be expected to exert great influence on their behalf, but on this occasion they were able to choose one of their own body. George Fitzhugh was a younger son of Henry, Lord Fitzhugh, and his mother was a sister of the great Earl of Warwick, the Kingmaker. He had been a Fellow of Pembroke under Booth, and in 1483 at the age of twenty-four had been appointed to the deanery of Lincoln. During his academic career the University with a complaisance characteristic of the age had exempted him from most of the acts and duties necessary for a degree, as well as from wearing academic dress and attending funerals. He seemed likely to be a useful patron, but from the College accounts he was at first an expensive resident. Wren notes that for the Foundress's Feast in the year before his election the cost was much greater than usual, because Mr Fitzhugh, Lady Fitzhugh and Lady Lovel were in College with their servants, and that at the same celebration in the following year while the Fellows had eight messes between them, two extra ones were provided in the Master's chambers for three ladies. Lady Fitzhugh, the Master's mother, gave vestments to the College chapel, and his sister, Lady Lovel, was the widow of that counsellor of Richard III, whom the popular rhyme names "Lovel the Dog".

The new Master did not inflict his expensive household on the College for long. Since in 1493 complaint was made against his retainers for damaging the architecture of Lincoln Cathedral by shooting at it with bolts, his absence may have been some relief to the Fellows. But expenses were also incurred by messengers to the Master, as when Mr Sewell was paid eighteen shillings for his journey to Lincoln and for his spurs. Further, the record of business done by the President increases, and quarrels seem to have arisen. Oliver Coren of Cumberland, the President, writes to the Master that he hears "you be informed of dyvers of yr friends at Cambridge that I presume to interpret the Statutes of Pembroke Hall your College; and not alonely that but also take upon me otherwise and more largely than it appertaineth to me".

He goes on to say that at the terminal reading of the statutes he himself had wished to refer to the Master for a definition of the President's powers, whereupon "some said, it needs not to disease the Master therein: for then would he think that ther were more trouble and division in the place, than is moved". Coren had then suggested asking Chubbes, now Master of Jesus, how he had interpreted the statute while he had been President, but some of the Fellows did not like consulting anyone outside the College, and so the matter dropped.

Yet Fitzhugh's Mastership witnessed prosperous years in the history of the College. Men who were afterwards to be distinguished still came to Pembroke, among them Robert Shorton from Jesus, later to be the first Master of St John's College and Master of Pembroke, and Charles Booth, later Bishop of Hereford, who incorporated from Oxford at the College of his distinguished kinsmen.

But the years of 1488 to 1505 are chiefly notable for the number of important benefactions, which they witnessed. In 1494 by the will of William Hussey, Lord Chief Justice, the College received a bequest with which they purchased a farm at Teversham. In 1496 Nicholas, the younger of the two brothers Skipwith, obtained for the College a rent-charge at Northill, near Bedford. Thomas Langton gave the College the Anathema cup in 1497, and left fifty pounds in his will. And Richard Sokburn must have given the Foundress's cup at about the same time. In 1500 Edward Story gave a farm at Long Stanton and another at Haslingfield, and rich vestments for the chapel. In 1502 Richard Fox, Bishop of Winchester, sent by the hands of Roger Laybourne, a Fellow of the College, fifty pounds for masses for himself and for John Davidson, his predecessor in his prebend in St Paul's. In 1503 by the will of Gerard Skipwith lands at Eltisley and at Waresley, and a rent-charge at Gamlingay came to the College, and in 1505 more lands in Cambridgeshire at Shelford, Horseheath, Borough Green and Whittlesford came by the will of William Atkynson. Over this last bequest there was some litigation; the lands had been acquired by Atkynson from Lady Willoughby, widow of a London knight, and Lady Bray, widow of Henry VII's architect, and for these two ladies the College was enjoined to pray.

THE FOUNDRESS'S CUP

The silver-gilt bowl bears the inscription:

✠ 𝕾𝖆𝖞𝖓 : 𝖉𝖊𝖓𝖊𝖘 : 𝖞ᵗ 𝖊𝖘 · 𝖒𝖊 · 𝖉𝖊𝖗𝖊 : 𝖋𝖔𝖗 · 𝖍𝖊𝖗 · 𝖑𝖔𝖋 · 𝖉𝖗𝖊𝖓𝖐 · 𝖆𝖓𝖉 ·
𝖒𝖆𝖐 · 𝖌𝖚𝖉 · 𝖈𝖍𝖊𝖗

The stem is inscribed:

𝖌𝖔𝖉 · 𝖍𝖊𝖑𝖕 · 𝖆𝖙 · 𝖓𝖊𝖉

THE ANATHEMA CUP

The name of the cup is derived from the inscription:

qui alienaverit anathema sit

Fitzhugh died at the end of 1505, and with only a short delay the College elected as Master Roger Laybourne, a former Fellow of the College, who now at the age of thirty-nine was Bishop of Carlisle. Three Fellows went off to London with the letters of election, to which Laybourne replied, that the College had had most eminent Masters but that in love and charity towards it he hoped that none of them could surpass himself. Of a noble Cumberland family, and obviously a man of outstanding ability, he had served his apprenticeship in affairs under Bishop Fox. He seemed therefore marked out for a great career. In the following year he came to College perhaps for the first time as Master, and the gardens were tidied up for his welcome. But in 1507 he died, and the College elected in his place his great patron the Bishop of Winchester.

Richard Fox, after a somewhat obscure early life, attached himself to the fortunes of Henry VII, when he was still only Duke of Richmond and an exile in Paris, and he became the chief adviser and minister of that king. Successively Bishop of Exeter, Bath and Wells, Durham and Winchester, he was in 1507 at the height of his great power and wealth. In begging him to accept the election and to take upon him the slight burden [*tantillum oneris*] of the Mastership, the Fellows doubtless hoped to benefit by that munificence, of which they had already had an earnest, but whatever hopes they may have had, they were not to be fulfilled. In 1509 they took the almost indecent step of establishing during his lifetime a regular commemoration for him at four fixed dates in the year as had been done before for the Foundress and for Henry VI, but in the following year there was some quarrel between them and the Master, in the course of which Fox threatened to resign. During these years he was already working on his idea of founding a College at Oxford, and Corpus Christi College was soon to absorb his attention. Finally, when in 1516 his piety revolted at the worldliness of his political life and he sought to retire to his diocese, and when a year or two later total blindness afflicted him, he resigned his Mastership of Pembroke. Wren notes that Fox left the College "subiratior", but for one of the Fellows he had some respect and affection, for in 1523 he arranged for Oliver Coren, then at Soham, to exchange that living for one near Winchester, so that Coren might become his Confessor.

The resignation of Fox marks the end of that series of Masters, great magnates in Church and State, which had begun with the sanction given by the papal bull of 1450 to the election of Laurence Booth. The number of great and worshipful clerks bred in the College during these fifty years is remarkable, and in 1495 the sees of Winchester, Salisbury, Chichester and Llandaff were all held by Pembroke clerks, while at Durham and at York were two future Masters.

CHAPTER III

THE REFORMATION

When Fox founded his College of Corpus Christi in Oxford, the statutes which he made for it showed him a patron of the New Learning of the Renaissance, and it may have been his reputation as such which caused Dean Colet to send to Pembroke from St Paul's his promising scholar, Thomas Lupset. Lupset, who was to become the friend of More and Erasmus and other leading spirits of the English Renaissance, made but a short stay at Pembroke and the College cannot claim any other leading scholar of the new movement; but under Robert Shorton, who succeeded Fox as Master, Pembroke became a nursery of the Reformers of the English Church.

Shorton, a Yorkshireman, was originally at Jesus College and was elected a Fellow of Pembroke in 1505; on the foundation of St John's College in 1511 he became its first Master. He was active in the supervision of the buildings and finance of that College, and in the contract which he signed for the chapel he stipulated that much of the work should be like that in the chapels of his two former Colleges, "or larger and better in every poynte". After five years he resigned his Mastership of St John's, and soon after Cardinal Wolsey's visit to Cambridge in 1517 he became Dean of his private chapel. Wolsey's star was now almost at its zenith, and Fox was retiring from public life; doubtless the fact that Wolsey was Shorton's patron weighed with the Fellows of Pembroke when they chose him as Master. He had also proved his ability in his Mastership of St John's. In the letter which they wrote to inform him of their choice there is an under-tone of their disappointment of the hopes which they had held of benefiting by the munificence of Bishop Fox. They had considered, they wrote, not so much age and wealth as manners and virtue, and that Shorton may be of no less benefit to the College by his carefulness towards it than anyone else by his riches, even if he be of great wealth. They also claim that Pembroke, like a careful nurse, had brought him up as her own child, though this claim might also have been made by Jesus.

He quickly showed his good will to the College. A few weeks after his election he conveyed to the College the manor of Chesterton Vescie in Huntingdonshire,[1] and two years later he acquired a property at Orton Waterville known as Rouse's, which eventually he gave to the College. In the first year of his Mastership the College was still further enriched by the gift of Sir Philip Bothe of certain house property in London. Bothe was of the same family as Archbishop Laurence Booth, but belonged to a branch of it which had settled in Suffolk. His kinsman Charles, who had joined Pembroke College on incorporating from Oxford in 1506, had been raised to the see of Hereford in 1516, and he was concerned with his brother in this gift, which was to endow three extra Fellowships, or two Fellowships and a bible-clerk. A few years later the College received a legacy under the will of Sir Roger l'Estrange, of the famous Norfolk family, who had been brought up in the College; with it was bought a farm at Barton in Cambridgeshire.

Shorton's influence with Wolsey was sufficiently great for the Cardinal to entrust to him the choice of promising Cambridge scholars to be Fellows of the great new college which he was founding at Oxford, and in 1525 the Master and Fellows of Pembroke agreed that John Clerk, one of their own Society, should hold his Fellowship for one more year, "his absence and his fellowship in the College at Oxenforthe notwithstanding"; they also agreed that should he wish to "forsake his said fellowship in the college of Oxenforde and [wish] to come again to abide within the said College called Pembrok Halle", the Master and Fellows would readmit him. But Clerk never returned to Pembroke; carrying with him to Oxford views which were beginning to fill the minds of the younger generation at Cambridge, he began to teach the new divinity, holding readings and classes in his own chambers. He soon became involved in a charge of heresy, and as a result of his treatment died in prison in 1528.

[1] This property was sold by the College in 1567, on which Wren comments "Eheu", and the proceeds applied to the purchase of part of the manor of Barway near Soham.

He has been claimed as the "first martyr" of Christ Church. Cambridge at this time, and Pembroke as much as any College, was in growing revolt against the old dispensation, and two of the senior Fellows of Pembroke, who had been elected under Fox, John Thixtill and George Stavert or Stafford, were among the prominent reformers. Thixtill's scholarship and ability were so well recognised that in the schools "Thixtill dixit" became a substitute for "ipse dixit", and Stafford's death was the result of an act of pious charity. He heard that one "Sir Henry", a conjurer suspected of practising the black arts, though he may have been a mere mathematician, was sick with the pestilence; he insisted on visiting him to pray with him, and was himself fatally infected. By his will he bequeathed books to the College library. Stafford died in 1529; John Bradford, who had been a soldier, and in 1540 was elected a Fellow of Pembroke, was with him as he lay dying, and among the B.A.s of the College in 1526 had been John Rogers, who was to be the first martyr of the Marian persecution. Nicholas Ridley had been elected to a Fellowship in 1524.

Another Fellow during Shorton's Mastership was William Turner, a pupil of Ridley, who like his tutor came from Northumberland. Leaving Cambridge to preach in 1540 he was imprisoned for his opinions, and the College in 1542 "ex dono benevolentiae" sent him twenty-two shillings and eightpence. He then turned to medicine and also began in England the scientific study of botany; in 1551 he published the first English Herbal. In the reign of King Edward VI he won preferment, and as physician and chaplain to the Protector Somerset was appointed Dean of Windsor without duty of residence. Another physician was Thomas Byll, Fellow in 1523, who had leave of absence in 1530 to travel and to study medicine in Padua. He became physician to Henry VIII and to Edward VI, and his brother was Master of Trinity College. Richard Cheney, who had been a scholar at Christ's College, was elected a Fellow in 1530, and after an active life in College became, after the accession of Elizabeth, Bishop of Gloucester.

Not all the Fellows under Shorton were supporters of reform. John Addison became a chaplain of Bishop Fisher, while Shorton himself had little sympathy with the new movement, and his attachment to Queen Katherine, whose Almoner he was, must have emphasised this difference. For when the king was seeking divorce from her, he was one of the few clerics who spoke in her favour in convocation. His resignation of the Mastership in 1534, the year after Cranmer had pronounced Henry's marriage with Katherine invalid and the year of the Act of Supremacy, may have been due to his position, although preferment still came his way and he was in the same year appointed Archdeacon of Bath. He left Pembroke, however, with no ill will, and on his death in 1535 he bequeathed to the College money with which a farm called Beaulies at Whittlesford in Cambridgeshire was purchased. How much he had resided during his Mastership it is impossible to tell. He had other preferments and offices which had calls on him, but he was a substantial benefactor and left the College at a moment when it was to begin once more to acquire a reputation as a breeding place of "good and worshipful clerkis".

Of twenty-one Fellows elected under Shorton eight came from the counties of Northumberland, Durham and Westmorland, and this may in some way account for the election of his successor. Robert Swinburne was from Northumberland, and a Fellow of Catharine Hall. During the three previous years he had been very active in University affairs, chiefly in one of those perpetually recurring struggles between the University and the Town. In 1533–4 he and Ridley, who was then Proctor, had been working together to preserve the privileges of the University and journeying together to London to plead the cause of the University at Court. But the choice of him as Master appears to have been disastrous, and Wren's account of his short reign is a long roll of his misdeeds, chief of which was what Wren calls a "foedissima abalienatio", the sale of Botolph's Hostel for fifty-five pounds. Thus passed out of the possession of the College one of Laurence Booth's chief gifts, which as time went on might have been the most valuable, the whole of the site between Pembroke Street and Botolph Lane.[1] Plate was also sold to the value of more than seventy pounds to carry out repairs and alterations to the buildings. A study was built in the Master's chamber, which suggests that Swinburne unlike Shorton meant to reside, the large

[1] The College has since the War bought back a portion of this site.

western window of the chapel shown in Loggan's print was made, and thirty-five pounds were spent on a wall round the orchard. Some of the plate seems only to have been pledged, for in 1536–7 Ridley redeemed some pieces for the College. It is, however, only fair to Swinburne to suggest that much of this expenditure may have been absolutely necessary, and that the times were particularly difficult for the Colleges. The Act of Parliament of 1536 "compelling spirituall persons to kepe resydence upon their benefyces" drew away from the University a class of men, who though they may have been detrimental to an atmosphere of hard study, "occupying such rooms and commodities as were instituted and ordeyned for the maintenance and relief of poor scholers", did contribute towards the expense of maintaining the Colleges. In 1540 the College found it necessary to let a portion of St Thomas's Hostel for a brewhouse, perhaps to replace the facility for brewing which they had lost by the sale of Botolph's Hostel, but more probably because there were no longer the students to fill the hostel. But another aspect of the hard conditions of the times may have encouraged expenditure. In 1535 the College accounts show an expense of £1. 2s. 4d. "For our Master's journey to London to deliver the Papistical Moniments", and this surrender of the ancient charters of the College to the king may well have increased the fear that spoliation was likely to ensue. Nearly three hundred and fifty years later fear that reserves might be confiscated stimulated the most disastrous orgy of spending in the history of Pembroke.[1] But whatever difficulties and doubts may have troubled the College under Swinburne's Mastership, it is hard to excuse the sale of the Botolph site, and there is other evidence that he himself was not untainted by the unscrupulousness which the uncertainty of the times was breeding. A kinsman of his, Rowland Swinburne, was Master of Clare, and to him he leased the next two presentations to Tilney, for a sum which does not appear to have ever been paid. He also presented to Saxthorpe and to Waresley members of other Colleges, one of whom was a northerner from Clare. There is also a letter from Sir Philip Bothe, which tells its own tale. Bothe was clearly not satisfied that his gift of an estate in London was safe in the

[1] See page 118.

possession of the College, and had stopped all rents from it until "some tyme as hys lernyd counsell and you have comunde together for the more surety of the londes", but he had been unable to get the College to send anyone to confer with him and his counsel, and "at that he toke grete dysplesure, and thought the College dyd monke wyth him". In 1537 Swinburne resigned, having been apparently presented to the living of Tilney by his kinsman, and there three years later he died. By his will he left forty shillings to repairs at Tilney and £6. 13s. 4d. to the poor there. He left books to two of the Fellows, Alanson of Northumberland and Briggs of Westmorland, and to the College he left "Hugh's works".

George Folberry, who succeeded Swinburne as Master, had been a Fellow of Clare and for a time master of the Grammar School at Durham. He is said also to have been tutor to Henry VIII's illegitimate son, the Duke of Richmond. His family had a generation earlier migrated south from the Northumbrian border to the East Riding of Yorkshire, and his will shows him to have been a man of some substance. He left money for the repair of Fowberry Tower, which stood five miles south-east of Flodden Field. To his servant he left a choice of his best geldings. There are also bequests of plate. To each of the Fellows he left one shilling, twenty shillings for a sermon, and forty shillings to be distributed among the poor and the priests on the day of his burial. He apparently died in College in December 1540, and was buried in Little St Mary's Church. He is said to have been renowned as a poet, but only a line and a half of his poetry have survived.

On Folberry's death the College elected as Master a third Northumbrian in succession. Nicholas Ridley had already proved himself in Cambridge a man of ability and force. An uncle had been responsible for his education while he was a scholar at Pembroke and, after he had been elected a Fellow, he had for a while studied abroad. Soon after his uncle's death he began to show his attachment to the reform party. While a Fellow he had been College Treasurer, and his experience too as Proctor had been more than usually valuable in bringing him into contact with the Court. His presentation by Cranmer to the vicarage of Herne in Kent in 1538 showed that he was already a marked man, and on the death of Folberry the Fellows wrote to him:

Postquam litteratissimus ille & litterarum amantissimus G. Folberrie Collegii nostri Præfectus apud superos esse desierat, animis nostris nobiscum pensitantes quam verum sit Christianissimi poetæ,

Domus orba magistro
Fluctuat ut navis, amisso in æquore clavo,

statim a sepultura Præfecti nostri, de eligendo novo Principe anxie & solicite cogitavimus.

And with much more in the same style they informed him that they had chosen him Master. He was quickly called upon to show determination in affairs of the College. There had been in the past several attempts by the Bishop of Norwich to contest the College right of presentation to the vicarage of Soham. Ridley, who had himself been presented to Soham, took the question before the Courts and obtained a decision in favour of the College. He saw to the proper investment of Shorton's legacy in the farm of Whittlesford and in 1549, on the suppression of chantries throughout the country, he obtained the freehold of that strip of land which belonged to the chantry of Little St Mary's Church, and separated the College from the rest of its property in Trumpington Street. It was at the same time that Corpus Christi College obtained the possession of Paschal Close, land belonging to a chantry in Great St Mary's and lying to the north of the College orchard, between it and the lane which is now Pembroke Street.

William Turner gave Foxe for his *Book of Martyrs* the following account of his former tutor:

Concerning his memory and his manifold knowledge of tongues and arts, although I am able to be an ample witness, (for he first instructed me in a further knowledge of the Greek tongue,) yet, without my testimony, almost all Cantabrigians, to whom he was sufficiently known, will and can testify....How able he was in confuting or overthrowing anything, yet without any boasting or noise of arms, not only I, but all with whom he disputed, easily perceived; unless he understood that they thirsted more after glory than was fit; for this he used to set himself more vigorously to crush. His behaviour was very obliging and very pious, without hypocrisy or monkish austerity; for very often he would shoot at the bow and play at tennis with me. If there were no other witness of his beneficence to the poor, I will testify this to all, that before he was advanced to any ecclesiastical preferment, he carried me along in company with him to the next hospital, and when I had nothing to give to the poor, besides what he himself according to his estate liberally gave, he often supplied me that I might give too.

Under Ridley's Mastership the reputation of Pembroke must have stood very high. During the sixteenth and seventeenth centuries migration between Colleges was most common, and more than one College can often claim the honour of the same worthy. Edmund Grindal, for instance, before he settled at Pembroke as Ridley's right-hand man had been for a time at both Magdalene and Christ's. John Christopherson was a witness of George Folberry's will in 1549, and in the following year a Fellow of Pembroke. But a year later he went on to St John's, became one of the original Fellows of Trinity, and under Queen Mary Master of that College and Bishop of Chichester. Nicholas Carr from Newcastle was originally of Christ's, migrated to Pembroke, and after being a Fellow went with others to the original Society of Trinity College, and became Regius Professor of Greek. Others spent all their time at Pembroke; notable reformers such as Edmund West, one of Ridley's own chaplains, and two who afterwards became heads of Oxford Colleges, Thomas Sampson, a doughty puritan, who was from 1561 to 1565 Dean of Christchurch, and Edmund Yeldard, who was the second President of Trinity College and held that office for forty years. Perhaps the most remarkable of Ridley's recruits as Fellows of the College was John Bradford. He had been a lawyer and a soldier, but converted by Sampson he came to Cambridge, where, as he said, Pembroke and St Catharine's Hall both wished to have him as a Fellow. He was elected at Pembroke in 1540.

Other famous Fellows and Scholars under Ridley were Anthony Girlington, the only Pembroke Public Orator; he died in College from eating too many custards; John Young, elected in 1550, afterwards Master and Bishop of Rochester and patron of Spenser the poet; Thomas Lorkin, later of Queens' College, Regius Professor of Physic; and John Whitgift. Whitgift, who had been a pupil of Bradford and of Gregory Garth, was elected a Fellow of Peterhouse, was Master of Pembroke for a short while in 1567 and then Master of Trinity from 1567 to 1577, and Archbishop of Canterbury from 1583 to 1604. Signs, too, of the confidence which was felt in Ridley in the outer world are to be seen in the matriculation at Pembroke in 1551 as pupils of Yeldard of two of the sons of Sir Anthony Denny, who had been one of the counsellors of Edward VI. On the first page of the first volume of the College accounts which has survived, in a list of those who in 1550 had not paid off the fee due on election as a Fellow instead of the statutory gifts in kind for the use of the high table, there appears the names of Bradford, Yeldard, Cheyney, Carr and Christopherson.

Whether Ridley resided any more than other Masters who were bishops, it is not easy to determine. Wren preserved from the College accounts references to his preaching at Soham, and payment for the hire of his horse to ride there, but that was before his promotion, and while he was contesting his right to the vicarage. He was also Rector of Herne in Kent, Chaplain to Cranmer and to the king, and in 1545 a Canon of Westminster. When in 1547 he became Bishop of Rochester he was allowed to retain his vicarages and his canonry, and all these duties must have kept him much away from Cambridge. After he became Bishop of London in 1550, he once held an ordination in College. During his absence Edmund Grindal seems to have been his deputy as President.

Ridley was Master during a period of great change. In 1547–8 the accounts record the purchase of an English Prayer Book and Bible. In 1546 the first of a series of Royal Commissions was appointed and returns of revenues and expenditure were called for. It is significant that the returns of all Colleges, except that of Magdalene, where the total revenue was only £43. 18s. 0d., show that expenditure exceeds revenue. The figures for Pembroke were: Revenue £171. 2s. 10d., Expenditure £183. 15s. 2d.,—

"sic expensa excedunt recept: £12. 12s. 4d." After which on the College copy of this return is written the naive comment: "Sic liber opus habet diligentiore examine, nam non est per omnia perfectus." One would like to be sure that this was written by the senior Treasurer for the year, Richard Hebb, who appears to have been something of a character. Wren records of him that "Vicarius fuit Sohamiae ubi eum etiamnum a posteris appellari memini 'Sir Hebb'. Hic ille est, ad quem in Theologia disputaturum (quod unicuique injunxerat Henricus VIII) Academia confluebat, ut riderent hominem. Sed partes suas sic egit, ut domum eum ad Collegium usque reducerent cum plausu."

In 1549 Edward VI sent another Commission, of which Ridley was himself a member. During this visit he actually lived in College, entertaining the Visitors to supper after their official visitation of the College on May 22, and on May 31, on their way back from Peterhouse, they came "thorow Pembroke Hall and herde a piece of a problem between Sir Mayhew and Hall". Mayhew was to become a prominent reformed divine and a translator of the Genevan Bible, and Hall to go over to Rome and end his life at Douay, and to be credited with the Life of Bishop Fisher. Throughout this visitation Ridley took a leading part in the discussions on points of doctrine which were staged for the occasion, and in which Grindal was one of the leaders for the reformed religion and John Young of Trinity, Lady Margaret Professor, defended the old faith. At the end of one of these debates Ridley, at the request of the other Commissioners, before a large audience of academics and courtiers, determined "scholastico more", while his audience stood bare-headed through the hour of his speech. He also supported the Fellows of Clare in their opposition to the proposal to join their College to Trinity Hall as a College for the teaching of civil law.

As a result of this Royal Commission new statutes were given to the University and to the Colleges. The changes which were made in the Foundress's statutes were not very great. Naturally the ancient "exequies", involving masses for the dead, were abolished, and the "obits" payable on these occasions became part of the annual wages of the Master and Fellows. The "minor scholars" were no longer to study grammar, that subject being

THE PROTESTANT MARTYRS

prohibited at the University and confined to the Schools. A Lecturer in Logic and Philosophy was established, and by a statute common to the University and Colleges to him with the Master and the Dean was entrusted the examination of all candidates for entrance to the College, the powers and status of the Dean being augmented in other respects also. The Foundress's statutes prescribed for certain decisions the consent of the "major et sanior pars" of the Society; this was now defined to mean the consent of the Master and at least two of the Fellows who by the ancient custom of the House were designated "Senior", as having power to admit their own sizars. The customary annual Feast on January 1 was allowed, but a second Feast on St Barnabas's day was suppressed in the interests of economy. For neither of these Feasts was there any statutory sanction. Unfortunately the beautiful name of the College "Domus sive Aula de Valence-Marie" was replaced by "Collegium sive Aula Mariae Valentiae".

Ridley had now become one of the chief churchmen in the kingdom. It is said that a sermon which he preached before the king in 1553 on the poverty in London was the first cause of the foundation of St Thomas's, Christ's and Bethlehem Hospitals. Nevertheless, when he paid a visit to the Princess Mary to offer to preach to her, she sternly refused to hear him. He was already being proposed for promotion to the see of Durham in his native north country, with Grindal named as his successor at London, when the death of the young king threw all things once more into disorder. By a sermon when the news of the king's death was still being kept secret, in which he had referred to the Princesses Mary and Elizabeth as illegitimate, Ridley hopelessly committed himself to the cause of Lady Jane Grey, and his prominence as a reformer marked him out for immediate attack. At Framlingham Castle he sought out Queen Mary and threw himself on his knees before her, begging her pardon, but she turned coldly from him, and he was committed to the Tower.

Every effort was made to procure a recantation from him so as to avoid the extreme course of law against him as a heretic. When he had been transferred to prison in Oxford, divines were sent to dispute with him, among whom was John Young, already his successor as Master of Pembroke. He refused to give way, and on October 16, 1555, he and Latimer were burnt at Oxford. In the long farewell which he wrote from prison while waiting for the end, there is a moving passage about his old College.

Farewell Pembroke Hall, of late mine own College, my Cure and my charge: what case thou art in now God knoweth, I know not well. Thou wast ever named since I knew thee, which is now thirty years ago, to be studious, well learned, and a great setter forth of Christ's gospel, and of God's true word; so I found thee, and blessed be God so I left thee indeed. Wo is mee for thee, my own dear College, if ever thou suffer thyself by any means to be brought from that trade. In thy Orchard (the walls, buts, and trees, if they could speake, would beare me witnesse) I learned without booke almost all Pauls Epistles, yea and I ween all the Canonicall Epistles, save only the Apocalypse. Of which studie although in time a great part did depart from me, yet the sweet smell thereof I trust I shall carry with me into heaven: for the profit thereof I think I have felt in all my lifetime ever after, and I ween of late (whether they abide now or no) there was that did the like. The Lord grant that this zeale and love toward that part of Gods word, which is a key and true commentary to all the holy Scriptures, may ever abide in that Colledge so long as the World shall endure.[1]

When Ridley wrote this farewell, of his pupils and colleagues at Pembroke Hall Rogers, the "protomartyr", and Bradford had already suffered at Smithfield; Grindal, Turner and Sampson had escaped abroad; Edmund West, one of his chaplains, recanted, but died soon after, it was said of a broken heart.

A College legend persisted till the seventeenth century that the Fellows refrained from electing a successor to Ridley until he was martyred, but Wren found from the College records that this

[1] The walk along the north side of the Fellows' garden is still known as "Ridley's Walk". A portrait painted in the eighteenth century from an old engraving was presented to the College by Richard Attwood, Fellow 1703 to 1735, and hangs in the Hall. In the Master's Lodge there is a contemporary portrait, which with a chair reputed to be his was bequeathed to the College in 1928 by the widow of Holt Waring Ridley, a collateral descendant.

was like many other College legends. For by March 1554 John Young of Trinity, the Lady Margaret Professor, and in that year Vice-Chancellor, had been elected Master. He was one of the most active of the heads in restoring the old faith and ritual, but many of those who had been Fellows under Ridley stayed on under him: John Young his namesake, who was afterwards Master; John Robinson, who was to be chosen first President of St John's College, Oxford; Robert Patchett, later Vicar of Tilney and a College benefactor who in 1568 gave forty pounds to provide fires in hall on Sundays and feast-days known as "commenti fires"; William Chaderton, afterwards President of Queens' College and Bishop of Lincoln; and John Bridges, Bishop of Oxford.

Old practices and ritual were restored; the Treasurer's accounts show that the St Barnabas's Feast was held, that there were bon-fires on Midsummer Eve and St Peter's Eve, and the bible-clerks were paid 4d. for watching upon Christmas Eve. A new Com-mission was appointed to visit the University and ensure the re-establishment of the old faith. The diary of John Meres, the Beadle, shows John Young very prominent in the University at this time, dining out and entertaining in Pembroke the learned Doctors of the University and their wives. On January 1, 1557, Meres dined at the Pembroke Feast: "Benet Prime and his men being ther and playd and not the towne Waytes. Ther came no poore people ther for awlmes." On January 2 "sone after vii they [the Commissioners] went to Pembroke Hall and they were receyved as before and so dyned and continued there untill iiii of the clocke...Feb. 10. Mrs [i.e. Magistri] Garth, Girlington, and Yonge [i.e. Young, the Fellow] sent for again, upon accounte; D. Younge [the Master] sente for againe and as it was thowggte put in dawnger of the loss of his lector and mastershyppe."

The difficulty about the accounts seems to have been due to the discovery of a debit balance on the commons account, for which the Fellows should have been held responsible, but Young and his supporters must have had some fun out of these interviews with the Commissioners. One of them was John Christopherson, once a Fellow of Pembroke, but by that time Master of Trinity and Bishop of Chester, whose debt for his "introit" on election to his Fellowship was still shown in the accounts as an unpaid debt due to the College. The debt is heavily crossed through in the accounts, and it would be interesting to know if this correction was made before or after the book was produced before the Commissioners.

In 1557 bonfires were once more blazing, this time to welcome the proclamation of Queen Elizabeth, the College buys "psalters in Englyshe" and still another Commission was sent down to re-enact the oath of supremacy. This Commission re-enacted the statutes of Edward VI with some slight changes and by these statutes the College continued to be governed till Queen Victoria's reign. John Young was removed from his Mastership; the Fellows, however, even in writing to Edmund Grindal to offer him the Mastership speak in high terms of Young:

excellentem & in omni literarum genere admirandum hominem, & nobis sane iucundissimum, qui eam [sc. domum] etsi incredibili pietate complexus est & celeberrima quidem fama sui nominis & doctrinae vehementer cohonestavit, una re tamen maesta fuit, per hoc tempus maiorem in modum, quod proprium maluit alumnum habuisse, a quo regeretur, quam externum.

Young soon found himself in prison, first in London at the Fleet, and afterwards at Wisbech Castle, where he remained till his death about 1580. He is held by some to have been the real author of the Life of Bishop Fisher generally attributed to Richard Hall.

Grindal, who was about to become Bishop of London, hesitated to accept the Mastership. It may have been that he was uneasy about the plurality, but perhaps he may also have thought that what was said about Young in the letter inviting him to be Master, by some who had been with him Fellows under Ridley, did not augur well for stability. The College thereupon begged the intervention of the Visitors to persuade him to accept: "Detulimus vero ei inane nomen Principatus in quo solicitudinis, curae, laboris, aliquantulum est; emolumenti plane nihil." Grindal's hesitation was overcome, but during the three years of his Mastership he never entered the College. Yet he kept a watchful eye over its interests and was to prove a very substantial benefactor.

He seems to have been uneasy about his position, and in 1561 he already thought about resigning, when the Master of Trinity recommended to Burghley the Chancellor either John Robinson of Pembroke, afterwards first President of St John's, Oxford, or Matthew Hutton of his own College, the Lady Margaret Professor of Divinity. Hutton was one of Grindal's chaplains, and when Grindal resigned in 1562, Hutton was elected Master. He was a moderate and equable man; in the acute controversy about the wearing of surplices he was one of the heads who recommended a compromise, much to Matthew Parker's disgust. He was a real scholar and in 1562 became Regius Professor of Divinity, and as such led the theological disputation before Queen Elizabeth, when she visited Cambridge in 1564. It was probably on this occasion, perhaps after Bridges, then Dean, had made her a Latin oration at the College gates, that the Queen apostrophised the College with "O Domus antiqua et religiosa". Hutton was, however, marked for promotion, and in 1567 on his appointment as Dean of York he resigned. Subsequently in 1589 he became Bishop of Durham, and in 1596 Archbishop of York, the fourth and last but one of the Masters of Pembroke to attain that dignity.

The College again applied to Grindal to suggest a successor, and he recommended John Whitgift, another of his chaplains, who was still a Fellow of Peterhouse. The College duly elected him in April, but in July he was elected Master of Trinity, from which office he was, like his two predecessors as Masters at Pembroke, finally to reach the throne of an archbishop.

Once more the College turned to Grindal for advice, and elected another of his chaplains, John Young. A Fellow in the last year of Ridley's Mastership, Young had remained in the College under the Mastership of his namesake, being Treasurer at the time when the Commissioners were investigating the College accounts, but in 1563 he had left the College for a living in London. In 1567 he was Rector of St Magnus the Martyr, London Bridge, and a prebendary of both St Paul's and of Southwell, and in 1572 he was appointed a Canon of Westminster. Following the example of his patron Grindal he does not appear to have resided in College to any great extent. In the first year of his Mastership he was out of commons for twenty-two weeks, but during the following year when he was Vice-Chancellor and must have been in Cambridge on some occasions he is granted an allowance for the whole year in lieu of commons, and this allowance is made "praefecto aegrotanti". It is impossible therefore to estimate from these allowances for commons the extent of his absence from Cambridge, but there is direct evidence of his non-residence in the letters of Gabriel Harvey.

These letters give an amusing picture of Pembroke during the spring and early summer of 1573, at a time when the poet Spenser was still at the College. The Fellows of Colleges were only just recovering from their indignation at Whitgift's *coup d'état* in 1570, when by rapidly procuring new statutes he established the Heads of Houses as a definite estate in the academic republic with almost absolute control of its affairs in their hands, and with an absolute veto on the proceedings of their own Colleges. This change took the power out of the hands of the *regent* Masters of Arts, that is the Masters of Arts during their first six active teaching years, and put it in the hands of the Heads and the Caput.[1] There was consequently some stubborn hostility against the Heads of Colleges. One of the leaders in opposition had been Lancelot Brown, of Pembroke, of whom and his adherents the Heads complained that they did "not only go verye disorderlie in Cambridge waring for the most part their hates and continually verie unseemlie ruffes at their handes and greate Galligaskens and Barreld hoose stuffed with horse Tayles with skabilonions and knitt netherstockes to fine for schollers; but also most disguysedlie theie goo abroade waringe such Apparell even at this time in London (although like hypocrites they come at this time outwardlie covered with the scholler's weed before your honors) that a great sorte of godly men and such as bear good will to the university are greatlie offended to se such unseemlie going of schollers and especially of Proctors and ministers (through whose lewde en-sample and behaviour the universitie is evell spoken of and poor schollers lesse respected)". Brown had been at St John's College till he took his M.A., and had come to Pembroke for the study of medicine: he was destined to live down this reputation for

---

[1] The *caput senatus* consisted of the Chancellor, three Doctors, and two Masters of Arts. It was replaced by the Council of the Senate in 1856.

disorder and to become physician to both Queen Elizabeth and King James. Though he was not elected a Fellow of Pembroke till 1567, he was in age one of the elders in a rather young Society. The senior Fellow, "Mr Praeses", who as the Master's deputy ruled the Society in his continual absence, was Thomas Nuce, one of the translators of Seneca's *Octavia*.

Of the same seniority as Brown was Humphry Tyndall, who had been at Gonville Hall and Christ's College before his election to a Fellowship at Pembroke. Among the five junior Fellows were Thomas Nevile and Gabriel Harvey. Harvey was, to use the end of one of his own execrable English hexameters, a "passing singular odd man", and he had offended the greater part of his colleagues by his conceit, and because "he was not familiar like a fellow and did disdain every man's company", that for instance he "needs in al hast be a studdiing in Christmas, when other were a plaiing, and was then whottest at mi book when the rest were hardist at their cards". On these grounds and others they refused to pass his supplicat for his degree of Master of Arts, and Harvey wrote to the absent Master to complain. The leaders against him were Thomas Nevile and Osburn the tutor. Against Nevile, Harvey retorts a *tu quoque* for "a write patern of a noble stummock", "for it were nedles for me to go about to point out his pride and lustines, wheras his oun gai gallant gaskins, his kut dublets, his staring hare, with sum other gudli and gentlemanlike ornaments, do and wil discri it sufficeently." Harvey's defence was "that at usual and convenient times, as after dinner and supper, at commenti fiers, yea and at other times too, if the lest occasion were offrid, I continued as long as ani, and was as fellowli as the best. What thai cale sociable I know not: this I am suer, I never avoidid cumpani: I have bene merri in cumpani: I have bene ful hardly drawn out of cumpani". Young wrote to Nuce, his deputy, but apparently the peremptory tone of his letter offended "Mr Praeses", who "tuke it in marvelous great duggin that your worship had writen so sharply and bitterly unto him as he thought". Nevile had now won over the two junior Fellows, Flower and Lawhorne, and "the yung cockerels, hearing thes ould cocks to crow so lustely, followid after with a cockaloodletoo as wel as ther strenhth wuld

suffer them, and, thouh not in lowdnes yit in hardines, showid
them selvs chickins of the game". Brown also on his return to
College joined in the faction, supported by a pensioner named
Gawber, who was studying medicine. Brown was probably
moved more by the Master's offence to Nuce and his own general
hostility to the new statutes than by any dislike of Harvey. The
Master in a letter to Tyndall, who was favourable to Harvey,
advised a policy of delay, and poor Gabriel was almost in despair:
"Stomachatur Osburnus; Nevellus furit; Flowerus Lawhernusque
indignantur; et postremo Nucius atque Brownus nescio quid
monstri alunt."

But Young knew how and when to act. At Whitsuntide, after
this storm in a teacup had been raging since the week before
Easter, he suddenly "cam downe himself to Cambridg uppon
Thursday in Whitsunweek being the xiiii day of Maye, for no
other purpose that any could persaive but only to stench this
strife, and rid me of trubble". The Master himself put the grace
for Harvey's degree through to the Senate, and though Gawber
tried to non-placet it as not having passed Harvey's own College,
it was carried. The Master then "admonished" Osburn and
Nevile, and ordered Tyndall to put Gawber out of commons.
Harvey writes exulting to his father: "And as for gentle M.
Gawber, his Mastership may go shake his eares elswhere, and
bespeake his diet at sum ordinary. Pembroke Hall fare is not for
his tooth. The truth is, our Master chargid him to be packing,
and willid M. Tyndall to put him out of Commins, and indeed
so he is, I warraunt him, although otherwhiles he lingereth about
ye Colledg like a masterles howne, bycause he wuld not seem to
be thrust out: but indeed looketh like a dog that has lost his tayle,
or to make the best of it, like an unbedden guest that knows not
where to sitt him downe." The Senior Proctor, Walter Allen
of Christ's, crowned Harvey's triumph by putting him at the top
of the list of seniority for the year.

But the trouble was not yet over. The Master returned to
Cambridge for the statutory election of College officers on
October 10 and for the Audit. He caused Harvey to be elected
Greek Lecturer, but when he wished to hold an election of new
Fellows, Nuce, Jackson, Osburn, Brown and Nevile all refused

to vote because, "thos that were now fellows had not bene usid like fellows", and because the Master had "forcid mens voices". They also challenged the legality of the "admonitions". On this point Young stuck firmly to his action, and said "he would not revoke it for a thousand pounds, bycaus he knew he should do very ill if he did so. Thei urging that it could not tak place, he said it could, and should take place; offering to pawne an hundred pownd to five pownd, if the matter were hard of ani wise judg in Ingland".

But after he had gone back to London, Gawber was ominously brought back to the Fellows' table, and Brown, who was now Junior Proctor, when Harvey was just about to begin his first Greek lecture in the College hall, where Spenser and Andrewes may have been present, "cummith swelling in, like sum greater man then the Junior Proctor, and commaundith the schollers from the table; saiing in his Proctors vois that I shuld read no lecture there; as he bi his Proctoral autoriti had suspendid me before, and I as yit had not been absolvid". Brown had of course no special standing as Proctor inside College as Harvey notes: "But if he wuld but take the chainid book in his hand whitch his man carriith after him, and take the pains to run over the title concerning the Proctors office, I beleev he shuld find his autoriti wil scars stretch so far as to order, or rather disorder, matters at his pleasure, and to others shame, in private collegis."

After this scene Harvey, on Nuce's advice, refrained from any further attempt to lecture, and three weeks later wrote to the Master complaining that the scholars should have no Greek lecture in the College of Ridley, Grindal, Bradford, Carr, Girlington and Hutton, and begging the Master to compose these differences so that "we shall al go quietly and rowndly to our books, and so in time grow to that ripenes of lerning, wisdom and eloquens whitch thos our predecessors grew unto, that at length it mai pass for a gud consequent he is a Pembrook Hal man, ergo a good schollar".

Harvey seems soon after to have been reconciled with his colleagues, and he held office as Bursar and as Treasurer. But he was restless and ambitious, and in 1578 when by the statutes he had to apply himself to the study of divinity, but himself desired to study law, he could not even with the support of the great Earl of Leicester and of William Fulke, by that time Master of Pembroke, persuade the Fellows to allow him to retain his Fellowship. Leaving Pembroke he was elected to a Fellowship at Trinity Hall, and there he was in 1585 actually elected Master, but "her Majesty's mandate over-ruled the case". Later he and his brother, Richard, also of Pembroke, were involved in a controversy with the poets Greene and Nashe, which became so virulent that in 1599 the government suppressed the writings of both Harvey and Nashe. He had the year before once more failed to secure Court favour for his election as Master of Trinity Hall, and had already, it would appear, retired to his birth-place, Saffron Walden, where, till his death in 1631, he practised astrology and medicine.

Gabriel Harvey's greatest fame, however, is that he was Spenser's friend, though he tried to persuade Spenser to cramp his natural genius with classical metres. Spenser matriculated at Pembroke in 1569, having come up from Merchant Taylors' School. He took his B.A. in 1573, and was placed eleventh in the order of seniority. The College Admission Book does not begin till 1616, and the only documentary evidence we possess of Spenser's presence in College is to be found in the Commons accounts, where on four occasions there are recorded payments to him *aegrotanti*. This has been taken as proof that he suffered ill-health while he was at Cambridge, but with the example of the allowance to John Young as "sick" throughout the whole year of his Vice-Chancellorship, there seems some doubt whether these *aegrotats* were genuine. Moreover, two of Spenser's absences cover the six weeks of Lent in the year 1572, and during that period all the scholars and some six or seven of the Fellows receive the same allowance and there is evidence that *aegrotat* allowances during Lent were an established custom, while the last time Spenser's name appears is for the last six weeks of the academic year 1573-4, when owing to a very severe outbreak of the plague in Cambridge the University was practically disbanded in the late summer, and the College accounts begin in the October following with "Allowed for 7 fellows for their commons in the plage time" and "It. 8 pueris in the time of the playg 13 weeks".

EDMUND SPENSER

When in January the University once more assembled, the Fellows to console themselves for having missed their usual "exceedings" at the Commemoration of Benefactors in the week of All Saints altered the calendar, and the week before Ash Wednesday is called "the week of All Saints". Spenser probably did not return to Cambridge, and a few years later, when John Young became Bishop of Rochester, he was employed in his household.

Two names appear fairly frequently in these somewhat suspicious *aegrotats*, those of "Androse" and "Dove"; in one year Dove receives an allowance in respect of a total of fifty-two weeks. Lancelot Andrewes and Thomas Dove both held the newly established scholarships on the foundation of Thomas Watts, Archdeacon of Middlesex. Watts had been a scholar at Christ's College, and was one of Grindal's chaplains. When in 1570 Grindal was promoted to be Archbishop of York he urged as one of the causes for his delay in going north to his province, that he wished to see through a grant of mortmain to Pembroke Hall. This was to enable them to receive Watts's gift of farms at Ashwell and Sawston for the endowment of seven Greek scholarships in the College. Grindal himself had already before 1568 given to the College a tithe of forty shillings for the payment of a Greek Lecturer. The establishment of scholarships is the usual type of benefaction during this period, though the scholarships were often tied to some school, as for instance the scholarship founded in 1568 at Blackrode School by John Holmes of London, citizen and weaver, for a scholar to come to Pembroke. Watts's scholarships were not attached to any school, though preference was to be given to Londoners, with a second preference to the counties of Yorkshire and Lancashire. He drew up an elaborate code for the duties of his scholars. They had to declaim in their turn in Latin and in Greek on some moral or political question chosen by the Master or his deputy, the declamation to be pronounced by heart, but also written out in their own hands, and one of the qualifications for election was ability to "write fair". They had also to compose Latin and Greek verse epigrams on some topic taken from the scriptures appointed to be read on Sundays and Festivals, to write them out in their own hands and set them on the screens before dinner. Before election the scholars were to be examined in Latin, Greek and Hebrew, and the College was to choose none but "of good hope and towardness for witt and memory: like to continue in the course of learning: well affected towards religion and the ministry ecclesiastical".

The value of this benefaction in attracting able boys to the College is to be seen in the list of those who held the Watts scholarships. Between 1571 and 1636 eighty-three names are recorded, and thirty of these succeeded to Fellowships. Lancelot Andrewes is the only one who became Master of Pembroke, but two became Masters of other Colleges, Matthew Wren of Peterhouse and Roger Andrewes of Jesus. Five of them became Bishops, Andrewes, Wren, Dove, Field and Puleyn. Altogether fifteen are included in the *Dictionary of National Biography*, including Crashawe the poet and Roger Williams, who founded the colony of Providence in Rhode Island. As far as can be traced at least seventeen of these eighty-three scholars came from Merchant Taylors' School, and six from the Charterhouse. Watts died in 1577 and by his will he added to his previous benefaction a legacy of sixty-eight books for the library. In 1578 John Young was promoted to the see of Rochester, resigned his Mastership and married the widow of Archdeacon Watts; finding that the College owed her arrears of an annuity out of the property given to the College by her former husband, he persuaded her to acquit the College of the debt.

On Young's resignation the Fellows were unable to decide, in choosing his successor, between Humphry Tyndall and Thomas Nevile, so they fell back on the recommendation of Elizabeth's favourite, the Earl of Leicester, and elected one of his chaplains, William Fulke. Tyndall became President of Queens' and Dean of Ely, and there is a legend that he was offered the crown of Bohemia; Nevile became Master of Magdalene, and then Master and great benefactor and builder of Trinity, as well as Dean of Canterbury.

William Fulke had been a Fellow of St John's College and a strong and restless puritan teacher. Once when he was deprived of his Fellowship for the extreme character of his opinions, he continued to lecture in the Falcon Inn and attracted many students. In 1570 he had been under consideration for the head-ship of his own College, and had been consoled for his failure by the patronage of Leicester and presentation to the living of Dennington in Suffolk. The long list of his writings shows how untiring he was as a controversialist. He was married and his views cut him off from the preferments which had been the reward of his predecessors in the Mastership of Pembroke, and the stipend of the office was therefore raised. He seems to have been much more regularly in residence, and he signs the accounts at the Audit in almost every year of his Mastership. Whether it is to be attributed to him or to Lancelot Andrewes as Treasurer is not clear, but in 1580–1 the accounts show signs of a considerable effort to reform and tidy up the College finances. In Andrewes's neat hand for the first time the Commons account is divided into four quarters, and some attempt is made to call in a number of arrears and irregular debts.

Wren, who probably had from Andrewes first-hand informa-tion of the College at this period, says that Fulke took great delight in increasing the number of undergraduates, a policy which Wren rather decries, since it entailed a larger increase in the number of Fellows than the endowments of the College warranted. To meet the difficulty of housing these increased numbers, Fulke in the year after his election persuaded the College to rebuild the hostel, which by a confusion which runs through the history of the College site they called University Hostel, instead of St Thomas's. Out of the rents from the rooms in it new scholarships were to be endowed, and Fulke himself gave £20 towards the cost. The College, however, seems to have been rather the loser by this scheme.

During Fulke's Mastership other new scholarships were founded. In 1579 William Marshall, Esquire, described as "servant of Archbishop Grindall", gave to Clare, Pembroke and Jesus Colleges equal shares of a rent-charge on lands at Brantingthorpe in Leicestershire to maintain a scholar at each of the three Colleges. It was, however, some years before the Colleges enjoyed this benefaction, and then after considerable legal expense. In 1583 Grindal, who had been translated from York to Canterbury, died after three uneasy years as Primate, and by his will founded an additional Fellowship and two more scholarships for those who had been educated at the grammar school which he also founded at St Bees in Cumberland. He also left to the College books, and a cup which had been given to him by Queen Elizabeth. In 1586 Mistress Jane Cox, widow of Richard Cox, Bishop of Ely, endowed with rent from lands in Boxworth a scholarship in memory of her first husband, William Turner, the botanist.

In 1589 Fulke died and left to the College a cup known as "the Nutt". During his Mastership and that of his predecessor a number of distinguished men had passed through the College. Richard Greenham, the puritan divine, was for twenty-one years Rector of Dry Drayton, and Roger Dod, who married Fulke's widow was, under King James, Bishop of Meath. Of Fellows under Fulke three, Lancelot Andrewes, Nicholas Felton and Samuel Harsnett, were to become Masters of Pembroke and bishops. Others less renowned were Thomas Mudd and Ralph Rowley, both of whom apparently wrote plays. Mudd, who came originally from Peterhouse, was in 1583 confined in the Tolbooth for libelling the Mayor in a play; he was also a musician, and the College appears to have established a music lecture for his benefit. Rowley's reputation as a dramatist depends upon the testimony of Francis Meres, one of the first critics to record Shakespeare's greatness, but as Meres matriculated at Pembroke while Rowley was a Fellow, his praise of Rowley may be only College loyalty. Nothing is known of Rowley's plays. Whatever dramatic gifts he and Mudd had they do not appear to have been good at accounts, for in 1586 with Richard Harvey, Gabriel's younger brother, they were involved in considerable indebtedness to the College, which was gradually liquidated by the simple process of stopping their wages.

Another Fellow elected under Fulke was Anthony Greene. Born in Moscow, but coming young to England and being educated under Mulcaster at Merchant Taylors' School, he was one of the Watts scholars and held the office of Greek Lecturer, but at the end of 1593 plague broke out in Cambridge and the University dispersed, the Commons accounts showing the usual *aegrotats*. When, however, the other Fellows came back into commons Greene is still shown as *aegrotans*, and his *aegrotat* lasted

for nearly forty years until 1633, he being all the while in Bethlehem Hospital, suffering, as he himself complained, from
"tormenting by devils and extraordinarie and incredible unrest".
Others who should be mentioned are the historian John
Hayward, who was imprisoned for his indiscreet dedication of
a history of Henry IV to Essex; his fellow-collegian, Samuel
Harsnett, then chaplain to the Bishop of London, had "allowed"
the book and was threatened by the same anger of the queen.
Robert Hitcham, later a distinguished lawyer, Member of Parliament for Cambridge and King's Sergeant, was to be one of the
chief benefactors of the College during the seventeenth century.
The learned compilers of the *Alumni Cantabrigienses* ask about
Egremond Fox, who matriculated at Pembroke in 1586, "Can
this be Guy Fawkes?"

During the seventy years between the resignation of Richard
Fox and the death of Fulke the history of the College becomes
steadily clearer. A University statute of 1544 established a regular
matriculation, and though the College Admission Book was not
to begin for another seventy-two years, yet Venn's *Alumni*
makes it possible to trace many hundreds of members of the
College between 1544 and 1616. Under Grindal, Hutton and
Young the normal annual entry at the College seems to have been
between twelve and fifteen, Fulke raised this to an average of
twenty-four. In the return to Henry VIII the endowment of the
College is shown as £171. 2s. 10d.; by 1590 the average of
receipts has doubled.

The extant accounts of the College begin with a kind of cash
or audit book in the year 1550, and a continuous series of Treasury
accounts starts in 1557. From these it is possible to glean much
more information about the interior economy of the College,
as for instance to trace the evolution of the Fellows' "dividend",
and of the various "bags", or funds; the "ling bag" for the trade
in salt fish, the "salt bag", and the "wood bag", which gradually
became the "coal bag", and also "my ladies bag". There is even
for a while during poor Mr Greene's enforced absence "Mr Green's
bag", into which his allowance in lieu of commons is paid, and
from which the College occasionally borrows, when short of
ready money.

CHAPTER IV

THE SEVENTEENTH CENTURY

Since the accession of Queen Elizabeth the College had elected Masters, whose religious bias had been towards puritanism. Grindal's leniency to the puritan preachers and their "prophesyings" had brought him into disfavour with the queen. Hutton was one of those whose plea for conciliation in the controversy about surplices had drawn from Archbishop Parker the advice to Cecil, not to listen to a "bragging brainless head or two", and Whitgift, who had also signed this petition, had not at the time of his election to the Mastership of Pembroke adopted that *via media* which enabled him to play so great a part in consolidating the Elizabethan settlement. Young had been a chaplain of Grindal, and a friend of Archdeacon Watts, Fulke had by his writings earned the title of "acerrimus papamastix". Under Lancelot Andrewes, who succeeded Fulke in 1589, the College began to develop into one of the strongholds of the High Church party. During the sixteenth century Edmund Spenser, the poet of Platonical puritanism, had been one of the chief glories of the College; Richard Crashawe, the Catholic mystic, was to be the poet of the seventeenth century.

Andrewes had while a Fellow revealed that genius for teaching which was the basis of his great reputation as a preacher. When he held the office of Catechist in the College, not only members of the University but also the local clergy crowded to his weekly lectures. Teaching he obviously enjoyed, as was seen later, when as Dean of Westminster he made a point of taking classes of the Westminster scholars, and his teaching was based on real and exacting scholarship. His learning was remarkable, and his study methodical; he used to say of anyone who came to see him in the morning, "that he feared he was no scholar". While he was still a Fellow his abilities had brought him to the notice of great patrons, and to Sir Francis Walsingham, Elizabeth's great intelligencer, he owed his first preferment, a living in London and a prebend at St Paul's. From his father, a Master Mariner and Master of Trinity House, he had inherited a capacity for affairs to which the neatness of his accounts as Treasurer and as Bursar of the College give testimony. He had also a sense of financial honesty and a scrupulousness in advance of his age. His biographer, Henry Isaacson, claimed for him that he found the College in debt and left it with over a thousand pounds in the treasury. Unfortunately there is a gap in the Treasurers' accounts from 1596 to 1606, so that it is difficult to ascertain in what way Andrewes built up this reserve, but such figures as are extant confirm an increase of money in the "treasure-house" from £125 in 1589 to £726 in 1606. After his election as Master Andrewes continued to preach regularly in London and to carry out his duties at St Paul's and at St Giles', Cripplegate, and so he cannot have resided in College a great deal. But his presence at the Audit in almost every year of his Mastership is attested by his signature in the Audit Book, and in the same book there is evidence that he established various College funds on a sound basis; in 1614 it was claimed that while he was Master the "coal bag" had been so well administered that it paid an increment to the Fellows' dividend. It had become customary for the Fellow-Commoners on admission to pay £2 for a piece of plate, and, when Fulke died, several of these contributions were still in his possession. As one of Fulke's executors was Roger Dod, a Fellow, who soon married his widow, the money was easily recovered, but Andrewes's scrupulousness is reflected in an immediate College order that in future the admission money should be laid on a side-table when the Fellow-Commoner first came to dinner, and taken over by the Treasurer and put in the seal chest. His shrewdness was shown in his insistence that to give effect to Grindal's benefaction the College should hold a long lease of the Palmers-fields estate, rather than depend upon the annual payment of an annuity by the distant trustees of St Bees' School, and his detailed familiarity with the College estates is seen in a letter to Matthew Wren, fifteen years after he had resigned the Mastership, concerning a wish to help the College by buying off a rent-charge on their estates at Orton Waterville: "I would have you search in the Overton box in ye Treasure house. You shall find there

2 bundles (if I mistake not) one of ye manor itself ye other of Rouses."[1]

It is also claimed that when University and Town finally agreed to adopt the project, mooted many years before by Andrew Perne, Master of Peterhouse, of bringing fresh water from the springs at Trumpington to run into and cleanse the King's Ditch, that medieval fortification of Cambridge which had long become an open sewer, Andrewes arranged that a separate branch of what is now called the Pem should run through the small garden and across the backside of the College behind the hall.

The years from 1589 to 1605 were years when the University Registrary was, as Fuller writes, "so negligent, that as one saith, *Cum fuit Academiae a memoria omnia tradidit oblivioni*" [Fuller adds, "I can hardly inhold from inveighing on his memory, carelessness being dishonesty in public persons so entrusted"]. As a consequence of this negligence it is difficult to ascertain the number and nature of admissions to the College under Andrewes, but since Wren, who was an ardent admirer of Andrewes, criticised Fulke's policy of admitting large numbers, the paucity of Pembroke men who can be traced during Andrewes's Mastership is probably not due entirely to lack of records. Confirmation, however, of the high opinion held of the College under his government can be found in the admission in 1593 as Fellow-Commoners of two of the grandsons of the great Lord Burleigh, Chancellor of the University. Of twenty Fellows elected while he was Master, four became bishops—Ralph Barlow, Archbishop of Tuam, George Cooke, Bishop of Bristol, Theophilus Field, Bishop of Llandaff and of Hereford, and Matthew Wren, Bishop of Hereford, Norwich and Ely; Jerome Beale became Master of Pembroke, Roger Andrewes of Jesus, and Wren of Peterhouse.

Among other *alumni* were Francis Anthony the doctor, who invented a patent medicine or *aurum potabile*, and sold it successfully until he fell foul of the College of Physicians; Henry Isaacson, the chronologer and biographer of Andrewes; and Thomas Dempster, the Roman Catholic writer. A bird of passage

---

[1] The manor was the gift of Laurence Booth; "Rouses" was the name of the farm given by Robert Shorton.

who stayed but a short while at Pembroke was Thomas Eden, the famous Master and benefactor of Trinity Hall.

During Andrewes's Mastership the College received substantial benefactions. In 1598 through the intervention of a former Fellow, Richard Buckenham, William Smart, one of the "portmen" or "burgesses" of Ipswich, gave to the College a farm called Diggers at Wyverstone in Suffolk of a rent of fourteen pounds to endow an additional Fellowship and two scholarships from his native town, and after his death Ralph Scrivener, who had married his widow, added to this benefaction a rent of twenty-one pounds to endow four more scholarships from the same town. Smart also gave to the College a large collection of old manuscripts, which had originally come from the library of the great monastery at Bury St Edmunds.

In 1601 Andrewes became Dean of Westminster, and the time he had to spare for his College must have been still further lessened. On the accession of James I, at a time when the archbishops of both Canterbury and York, Whitgift and Hutton, were former Masters of Pembroke, Andrewes was summoned to the Hampton Court Conference, and he was one of the leading divines appointed to carry out the translation of the Bible. In this great work on what is now known as the Authorised Version, he had among his colleagues his brother Roger, and Roger Fenton, who had both been Fellows of Pembroke under him, and Francis Burleigh a former Watts scholar. He had already twice refused promotion to a bishopric, but in 1605 he accepted promotion to the see of Chichester and resigned his Mastership of Pembroke. Four years later he was promoted to Ely, and in 1619 to Winchester, but throughout the rest of his life he kept in close touch with his old College, through Nicholas Felton, and through Matthew Wren, who had come to the College through his intervention and whose election to a Fellowship had been the last act of his Mastership. He died on September 26, 1626, and by his will he left to the College the living of Rawreth, and a thousand pounds to establish an additional Fellowship, and to increase the value of the four senior Watts scholarships, of which he had himself been one of the first holders. With this bequest the College bought an estate at Pertenhall. He also left money for a dinner on the day of his death, a celebration now held on a day conveniently near to the deposition of his body in South-wark Cathedral. He also left to the College all the books in his library of which the College did not already possess a copy, and in the year after his death his secretary, Samuel Wright, was admitted to the College, and was for a while Librarian. Wright's beautiful penmanship is preserved in a copy of Andrewes's Devotions in Greek in the College library, and it was he who drew at dinner the picture of Andrewes, a copy of which by the Dutch painter, Buxhorn, hangs in the Parlour. Through Andrewes there also came to the College Whitgift's copy of the Complutensian Polyglot Bible.

Samuel Harsnett, whom the Fellows next chose as Master, owed like Wren his early preferments to Andrewes. He had originally matriculated at King's, but had migrated to Pembroke while still an undergraduate, and had been elected a Fellow in 1583. He and Andrewes held much the same theological views, and Andrewes, who must then have had a high opinion of him, presented him into the living of Chigwell in Essex. Harsnett's abilities also won for him the patronage of Bancroft, Bishop of London, whose chaplain he was, and it was in that capacity, which involved among other duties the licensing of books, that he had the misfortune in 1599 to grant a licence to John Hayward's *Historie of the reign of Henry IV*. Hayward, who had been contemporary with Harsnett at Pembroke, was indiscreet enough to prefix to his book a flattering dedication to the Earl of Essex. Queen Elizabeth, for whom the story of the deposition of Richard II was as a red rag to a bull, suspected treason; Hayward was lodged in the Tower, and Harsnett was also for a short while under a cloud. He had already won for himself a reputation as a controversialist by his *A Discovery of Fraudulent persons*, in which he had exposed one Darrel, a cheating witch-doctor, and in 1603 he published his *A Declaration of Egregious Papist Impostors*, another attack on frauds connected with witchcraft, and a book of which Shakespeare certainly made use. At the time of his election as Master he was forty years old, and obviously well regarded, but his Mastership was to prove a period of grave disorder and discontent and to end in open rebellion.

HIC IACET SAM= VELL HARSNETT QVONDAM VICARIVS HVIVS ECCLESIÆ PRIMO INDIGNVS EPISCOPVS CICESTRIENSIS DEINDIC NIOR EPISCOP⁹ NORWICENCIS= DEMVM INDIGNISSIM⁹ ARCHIEPISCOP⁹ EBORACẼN QVI OBIJT XXV DIE MAIJ ANNO DÑI 1631.

QVOD IPSISSIMVM EPITAPHIVM EX ABVNDANTI
HVMILITATE SIBI PONI TESTAMENTO CVRAVIT
REVERENDISSIMVS PRÆSVL

BRASS OF SAMUEL HARSNETT IN
CHIGWELL CHURCH

He was a widower, and at the time of his election he was given unconditional leave of absence, for "the attending on his lord the archbishop", and for "the looking to his children", and when, on Andrewes's promotion to Ely in 1607, Harsnett followed him in the see of Chichester, he was allowed to retain his Mastership with his bishopric. But the inconvenience caused by this concession became intolerable. "His absence was not like other Masters' absence, who keeping near Cambr. or att London had weekly intercourse of lettrs for directing and ordering of business, but he being 100 miles hence, much inconvenience has rose upon itt. poore schollers have binne fayne to send so farre of purpose for theire graces", and tenants "have binne forced to ride both hither and thither". In the summer of 1614 it was reckoned that he had not been near the College for over a year, and except for the Lent term of 1613, not above three or four weeks in five years. Besides when he did come into residence, the Fellows complained that the College was "exceedingly damnified" by his presence. "Being a Bishop and by reason thereof, being to keep state at his meales in his lodgings, ye College napery of very fayre diaper and damaske (reserved only for high times) is extremely worn and spoyled. It having been observed, when his men have most negligently stayned it, and wiped ther shoes wth itt, or worse." The plate also was "much worne, battered, and broken, and not carried up (as formerly was used) into ye treasury, in above a twelvemonth together, by cause either he was at home to use it, or not at home to see it done, and ye president nere looked after itt". His choice of a deputy was most unfortunately one Thomas Muriel, "a man of many unsound opinions, and of no Religious, or conscionable deportments in his Life and conversation". Muriel, in the Master's absence, imitated his overbearing manners: "Besides being Proctor he made both ye Cookes att once his men, and at his plaasure used them, and carried them about wth him, so that sometimes the kitchen was wthout a cooke a whole day together,...leaving the College but one poore scull boy to dresse commons."

Some relief might have been expected when in 1612 Muriel, on the death of Humphry Tyndall, was appointed to the vicarage of Soham, and after his year of grace resigned his Fellowship, but

Harsnett's choice of a new President was just as unpopular with the majority of the Fellows; John Poclynton "whom he fetcht from another College [Sidney Sussex] (as himself sayd) bucause he held some opinions wch himself well liked, & so deputed him before 10 of the seniors was much suspected by the Society from whence he came for some opinions wch he had maintayned... and on ye gunpowder day last he tooke exception at an oration made by one of our scholars, by cause he had (yet oratorlike) named Faux ye trayter, wth some termes detesting and execrating that matchless impiety, affirming that it was an offence of our Church to speak evil of any that are dead".

Poclynton adopted a policy of attacking his opponents by hitting at them through their pupils. Walter Balcanquhall had been elected into a Fellowship from a Scottish University, and had attracted to Pembroke one or two Fellow-Commoners from those noble families of Scotland, which had followed James to the English Court, and the Fellows complained that "having admitted into ye College a young gentleman the Sonne and Heire of Sr J. Spence", Poclynton "upon particular command by letter from the Mr, in a short space of time punished him above 30s. for not disputing in Latin at every meale, whereas at his Admission (wch they were well content for) they saw that he was but a very young Grammar Scholler, not able to talk Latin, much less to dispute; at the same time dispensing therein wth another Gentleman whom the Mr loved".

When in 1612 Harsnett had thought of resigning, and a rumour of this had reached Bishop Andrewes, he had written to the king's secretary, Sir Thomas Lake, that he had heard from Felton that Harsnett "waxing weary of his mastership of Pembroke Hall, intendeth very shortly to make it over to one who save that he hath forebid his turn (a man might say it in charity) many years hath (and this year especially) showed himself unworthy of such a place; one Muriel concerning whom the Sub-Almoner can very well inform you". Andrewes then pressed the claims of Nicholas Felton, who had the king's favour. "The better sort of Fellows do wish for him, and, as now it standeth, I might say the greater. But it is certainly intended by the bishop to make an election of Fellowships before he gives over, that shall be brought in only on condition to give their voices afterward as he shall afterwards appoint them. I write you for no end but only to set you about good works. And a blessed deed you would do if you should help the College (hitherto of good report) and a worthy Master, such as I hope Dr Felton would be; which otherwise is likely to sink and come to nothing, if it light not in better hands. Sir, I desire you for his sake, for mine, but especially for the College's to add this to the number of your good deedes, and prevent this evil, and be a means that a good house may have a good head, which I much desire, because then I shall be in hope once more to see that College, which other I am not like."

At the election of Fellows soon after there were stormy scenes. Alexander Bolde ventured to urge "but in Reverent, Modest and Honest manner that they might choose those of their own house, being very fit for the places". For this the Master sharply rebuked Bolde, and when Bolde complained that if speaking their minds in this business were not to be granted, he would rather be wholly silent, Harsnett called him a "stiffe saucy clowne". Alexander Reade, a learned senior Fellow, who had also offended the Master, "was willed to look for nothing in the College and with some shameful and violent terms urged to give over his studies and to betake himself to teach abroad in a school". Other Fellows who had opposed the Master or criticised his actions, Matthew Wren among them, had been put out of commons.

In 1614–15 Harsnett was Vice-Chancellor for the second time, and his conduct while in residence further exacerbated the feelings of the opposition. King James paid a state visit to the University, and Wren, Reade and Brownrigg "by consent of the University" were chosen to take leading parts in the "Philosophy Act" to be determined before the king, but Harsnett "sought all meanes to appoynt others, & wth disgrace to omit them & afterwards (even to ye last hour) forbore not many pretended occasions of discouragement to them therein". The question to be debated in this famous Act was whether dogs could make syllogisms, and this learned conceit was so played out before the wisest fool in Christendom, that all the disputants won credit by their vivacious arguments, especially Matthew Wren, who when the king, "whose mind was all the while upon Newmarket heath", inter-vened with an instance of the sagacity of his own hounds, replied promptly that his majesty's dogs acted "by prerogative". Harsnett's conduct on this occasion in discouraging the Fellows of his own House was set in a particularly ungracious light by the action of his predecessor. Bishop Andrewes, who was in the company of the king and witnessed the debate, was so pleased by the part played by the members of his own College that he made them each a present of twenty angels.

Already at the Audit meeting of this year, the anger of the Fellows had exploded. Poclynton, whose unfamiliarity with the College accounts had not deterred Harsnett from appointing him Bursar of the College, refused to render any accounts. The Fellows met after dinner in the Master's chamber and besought him by the statutes to do so, but he "holding up to mockery the intention of the statutes, the custom of the House, the good faith and solemnity of the place and cause of meeting, at last late at night dismissed the Fellows with nothing done".

For some time Wren and his chief supporters, Balcanquhall and Ralph Brownrigg, had been collecting material for a petition to the king against the Master. Their grievances when finally assembled ran to sixty-three articles, varying greatly in seriousness. Some seem frivolous, but others reveal a most unsatisfactory state of affairs. The most important are those which deal with Harsnett's mismanagement of the finance of the College, both directly and through his deputies. The reserves carefully built up by Andrewes had been dissipated, it seemed to the Fellows, by unwise purchase of land. Yet there is much to be said for Harsnett's action here. Seven hundred pounds in bags in the treasure-house were exposed to theft and breeding no interest were useless, and to put the money into land was wise. One estate which Harsnett bought may have been a poor investment; possibly it was not an altogether disinterested transaction. Fulke had bought for himself certain lands at Dickleburgh in Norfolk; these Harsnett bought from his heirs for the College, and to find the price the College used up its reserves and had in addition to borrow money, Dr Nevile, the Master of Trinity, helping them at this juncture. But it was not a good estate, and the Fellows complained: "What man will purchase for so much loss, as ye Bishop would put ye College to, to give 900li for lands (part whereof was copyhold and so both cumbersome and chargeable) that should yeald to themselves but bare 40li per annum?" But another investment of Harsnett, very much deprecated by the opposing Fellows, turned out of incalculable value to the College. A long lease was purchased of land belonging to Corpus Christi College between the orchard and what is now Pembroke Street, and this was the first entry of the College on a strip of land called Paschal Yard, which it was finally to acquire some 250 years afterwards, and upon which now stand the whole of New Court, the old Master's lodge and Pitt buildings.

Another means by which the Fellows complained that Harsnett had wasted Andrewes's reserves was in the erection of new buildings, although the Hostel which Fulke had rebuilt only fifty years before was falling into ruin once more. Here again Harsnett seems to have been right and the Fellows wrong. Numbers in the University and so in the Colleges were steadily rising, and more accommodation was needed, nor was the building of the new chambers a bad investment. Work had been begun in 1614, and by the Michaelmas term of 1616 two-thirds of the north wing of Ivy Court was complete, and out of the new rents of the rooms the College established a lecture *in litteris humanioribus*, probably because money bequeathed by Henry Farre, a Fellow, for that purpose had been used to defray part of the cost of the new buildings.

But though Harsnett's financial policy appears to have been sounder than the Fellows thought, or at any rate more justified in the event, the petition which they prepared for presentation to the king reveals a state of affairs which may very easily have alarmed them. Muriel, through whom Harsnett during his long absences had to act, was certainly neither scrupulous nor businesslike. Letters from the Lord Chancellor remained unanswered; leases and deeds were being lost; and there was grave suspicion that he, if not the Master, derived personal profit from some of the transactions over College business. More serious perhaps were the suggestions that this illicit profit extended to the sale of Fellowships. Some of these suspicions may have been based on mere gossip, as when the petitioners urge that the "Master in private counsel seriously advised one of the company to get money in his purse, if he looked for anything, for the only ready way now to get any living or promotion was to pay for it". But there were ugly suggestions of money passing for election to Fellowships and for the renewal of leases.

There can be no doubt that the continual absence of the Master, and the unsuitability, to say the least, of the deputies whom he appointed had together produced a thoroughly disturbed and unhealthy atmosphere in the College.

Early in May 1616 King James was at Thetford, and as on Sunday he came from church, where he had been listening to a sermon preached ["suo more"] by Balcanquhall, Wren fell on his knees before him and presented a petition signed by the greater part of the Society. He was supported by Balcanquhall, Reade and Brownrigg. The ground had been well prepared and the favour of the king already sought through several prelates and courtiers, among them George Villiers, the favourite just then rising into power and the son of a former member of the College. The king read the petition through, was astounded, and referred it to a hearing before commissioners. Wren and Balcanquhall continued to ply the influential at Court, and on June 28 after a four hours' hearing, in spite of all Harsnett's protests, the petitioners won their case. "Io Triumphe, vicit veritas, simplicitas, innocentia", as Wren wrote to a friend. A week later the Chancellor of the University, the Earl of Suffolk, handed to Wren Harsnett's resignation. With this in his pocket Wren hastened back to Cambridge, but kept the decision secret for a couple of days while he sounded the other Fellows; then he suddenly summoned a College meeting at which he secured the election of Nicholas Felton as Master. Felton wrote in accepting the office

My onelie desire is that whatsoever shall be needful uppon the sudden to be done in behalf of ye Colledge or myself it may be doen by your wisdomes so peaceablie as passed exasperations can beare with hope of better times. And untill for ye whole Colledg we may work pacem ex cujusque Jure we shall doe well to work

Jus cujusque e pace expecting both with pacience: the ayming at omnium pax to my conceivyng [?] becomes *you* and at cujusque Jus cum omnium pace becomes *me*. My hope is yr wisdome in ye desire of ye one, will provoke and binde and enable me in ye desire of the other.

Nicholas Felton came, like Andrewes, from seafaring stock. He had been an undergraduate at Queens' and migrated thence to Pembroke; he was elected a Fellow under Fulke. In 1616 he was a man of sixty years of age, with a living in London and a prebend in St Paul's, and he had a son a Fellow of the College. He appointed Wren as his "Mr Praeses" and with this appointment begins a new era in the history of the College. Wren was not only, as the struggle with Harsnett had proved him, a resolute and capable man of affairs, he was also a genuine antiquary, filled with a love of the history and traditions of the College. He had originally come to Pembroke through the intervention of Bishop Andrewes, who being present when the scholars from the Mercers' School to St John's College, Oxford, were being elected, and finding that Matthew Wren had been crowded out, procured for him a scholarship at his own College. Wren is probably the most important figure in the history of the College during the seventeenth century, although he was never Master. In 1616 he was just thirty-one and on his appointment as President he soon set out to put the House of Valence Marie in order. A proper register of admissions to the College was started, and another for inscribing the orders and decisions made at College meetings. Working carefully through the ancient deeds of the College, of which he made the first catalogue, he compiled biographical lists of the Masters and Fellows since the foundation, and since some of the original material upon which he worked has now disappeared, these lists have formed an invaluable basis for all subsequent research. His application to records had also its practical side. Nicholas Skipwith's rent-charge from Gamlingay had been for some years in arrears, and in 1617 Wren received three shillings and fivepence for his horse-hire in riding thither. Unfortunately his journey was fruitless. Another rent-charge over which there had been difficulties was that at Northill in Bedfordshire. Wren organised a visit to investigate that too, and, though the cavalcade of Fellows that rode over the land questioning the oldest inhabitants "amazed and amused" them, for some years afterwards that rent-charge, which has also since been lost, was more or less regularly paid. But perhaps Wren's most valuable work was in the College library. The manuscripts were numbered and catalogued, the cases and shelves repaired, and a proper Librarian was appointed, to the payment of whom the College applied the benefaction lately received from a former scholar, Gregory Downhall, who had been secretary to Lord Keeper Egerton. Wren himself compiled a list of benefactors to the library, to which he prefixed a double frontispiece. On each half of this was painted a laurel tree, one with yellow leaves on which were inscribed the names of deceased donors of books, and the other with green leaves for the names of benefactors still living. Modestly on a leaf near the bottom of the green tree he put his own name, and every year upon his birthday he presented a book to the library.

The new buildings, a bone of contention with the late Master, necessitated a rearrangement of the "backside" of the College, and Wren was appointed to negotiate with the town for the right to close by night the *venella* or bridle path leading to St Thomas's Leys between the College and the orchard. Hitherto the duties of porter had been carried out by a scholar or sizar, but this increase in the means of entering the College resulted in the appointment of the first College porter, Edward or Ned Wenham, the under-cook. At this time the senior cook was Christopher Green, two of whose sons became Fellows of the College, and a grandson of whom was a Fellow of Gonville and Caius and Regius Professor of Physic. The Butler was Thomas Nashe, whose beard the Elizabethan poet of the same name had already made famous. A son of this Nashe, the Butler, was also to become a Fellow of the College and a royalist divine.

Wren's organising work was not all done under Felton's Mastership, which was of less than three years' duration. In 1617 Felton had been appointed Bishop of Bristol, and had been allowed to retain his Mastership, but he was already marked for further advancement, and though the Fellows would have liked to retain him still as Master, Wren was warned by Andrewes that at the next step in Felton's promotion there was little chance of the king's allowing him to retain his Mastership with a more important bishopric. Andrewes advised the Fellows to make up their minds to choose a Pembroke man as his successor, and he had after dinner through the mediation of Villiers, now Duke of Buckingham, obtained the king's word "for one of their own". But a new division was making itself felt in the Society. Under Harsnett a common sense of injury had brought Wren, the disciple of Andrewes, into the same party as Ralph Brownrigg, whose puritan leanings had already brought him into trouble with the Heads. Now a sympathy in religious outlook made allies of Wren and Harsnett's hated deputy, Poclynton.

When the name of Felton was being talked of in connection with the vacancy in the see of Lichfield, a faction led by Brown-rigg, and composed chiefly of junior Fellows, set themselves to resist the election of Jerome Beale, the king's sub-almoner. They first tried to get a royal mandamus for the election of Richard Senhouse of Trinity and St John's, afterwards Bishop of Carlisle; they then approached various other divines, including the poet and satirist, Joseph Hall of Emmanuel, afterwards Bishop of Norwich. Finally they wrote letters accusing Beale of being an Arminian. On January 19, 1619, the king wrote from New-market: "Although we doubt not but your affection to your own house will be sufficient motive unto you to prefer ane of ye same society to the government thereof before any of another college, yet such is our gracious care therof yt we have thought fit to recommend unto you the choice of some man bred in your own House, when the Mrship thereof shall fall void, rather than any other...assuring ourself that you will be careful to make choice of such a man as shall be neither a Puritane nor Arminian." Wren's trusty ally Balcanquhall was on leave of absence repre-senting the Church of Scotland at the Synod of Dort, and Wren wrote off for his support in the fight for Beale. Brownrigg attacked by taking exception to certain Fellows; Parker he alleged was married, Poclynton held livings which disqualified him to retain his Fellowship. On February 10 Felton declared the Fellowships of three Fellows who had offered to resign, Parker,

Poclynton and Bathurst, vacant; this was a loss of two votes for Beale, and of one for his opposers. On the 21st Felton resigned the Mastership, and the Fellows proceeded to an election. For some reason Brownrigg and two of his faction were absent, but as on the first count only eight votes were given for Beale, there was not a majority of the whole Society. After a short adjournment however Thomas Boswell (later Medical Fellow of the College), who had been one of Brownrigg's party, went over to the other side, and the requisite majority for Beale was obtained. Two days later there arrived royal letters freeing Beale from any suspicion of Arminianism, and also forwarding the vote for Beale given by Balcanquhall and ordering that it should be counted. This vote bears the seal of the town of Dort, and is witnessed by the leading divines attending the synod.

Jerome Beale, originally of Christ's College, was a former Fellow of Pembroke, and he had assisted Wren in formulating the articles of the petition against Harsnett. He was sub-almoner and chaplain to the king and he was a strong adherent of the Court party. He seems to have resided more regularly than either of his two immediate predecessors, and under him there was for some years comparative peace in the College. Wren as President continued his tireless work on the College records, but he too was marked for promotion. In 1623 he accompanied Prince Charles as his chaplain on his journey to Spain to negotiate a Spanish match, and soon after his return he was elected Master of Peterhouse. But as religious and political differences throughout the country began to grow acute, Pembroke became more and more definitely associated with the High Church and Court party. In 1628 the whitewash was removed from the chapel walls, presumably that the old medieval paintings might once more be visible, and there were occasional quarrels between such High Churchmen as John Tournay, Crashawe's tutor, and the puritan William Fenner.

Though, however, the College was becoming increasingly royalist, the Fellows did not always welcome the intervention of the king's prerogative. Ever since Elizabeth's reign, the Colleges, jealous of their statutory right of "free and spontaneous election", had protested against the intrusion of Fellows by royal mandate, and as a means of combating this invasion of their privileges many of them had evolved a system of pre-election. Fellows were elected before there was any real vacancy, and their sponsors took a bond that they would not claim any emolument before the vacancy occurred. By this means a royal mandate could always be met by a statement that there was no vacancy. In 1629 the king's letters were received urging the "general report and well approved merit" of one Jasper Chomley of Corpus Christi College and recommending his election as a Fellow of Pembroke.

Writing with "all humble and reverent premisses" to the king, the Master and Fellows pleaded that they had in the past obeyed such mandates, whether proceeding from the king or the prince, and they regretted that this last request should "instead of our readie and wonted performance beget an humble deprecation and excuse"...."The generall good report and well approved merit of Jasper Chomley was it that induced your Majestie to direct unto us your Gracious letters for his preferment. And we wish with all our hearts that his fame were as really sweete in Cambridge as it was charitably conceived at Whitehall. But in the University it is most certaine that he the said Jasper upon the importunity of a worthy Court friend was by the Mr of Bennet College, wherein he was brought up propounded unto ye fellows of yt Societie, whom not one man no not his Tutor Sterne vouchsafed a voice. Yr Matie may therefore easilie conceive what credit another Societie can get by advancing him who was so much slighted in his owne College. Moreover it is notorious that once in a sodeine passion (which they say haunteth him often) upon verie slender provocation, wth a pen knife he dangerously stabbed one Sr Palmer in the bellie: So that without much feare and jeopardie, there is little hope of safe converse with a man of his morosity." Besides, four pre-elected Fellows "lie still in expectation of profits", and have a legal claim, so that if Chomley were thrust in, "the College would be rent in pieces with brawles at home and law-suites abroad".

There had for some time been a small discontented party with a puritan bias in the College, and they took this occasion to attack the Master, using a pre-election of some years before, when a kinsman of his had been pre-elected, as the basis of charges of misgovernment. Their petition resulted in the appointment of a Commission to look into the matter, and Samuel Harsnett, now Archbishop of York, found himself in the ironical position of presiding over a court which had to judge one of his successors in much the same position as that in which he himself had stood twelve years before. The Commission heard the evidence, and decided against Beale, depriving him of his Mastership. But the decision was never confirmed. The other Heads of Houses in Cambridge rallied to the support of Beale, and Dr Butts, the Master of Corpus Christi and Vice-Chancellor, took the matter up to Court, pleading that for Fellows to petition the Crown direct was a breach of the privileges both of the University itself and of its Chancellor. His intervention was successful, and after long waiting about Court he returned to Cambridge in great delight with pieces of the broken seal of the cancelled Commission.

Beale however died shortly afterwards, and Benjamin Lany was elected Master in his place. He was a Suffolk man, who like Beale came from Christ's College. His father had been Recorder of Ipswich and he came to Pembroke first as Smart Fellow. In the contested election of Jerome Beale he had been one of Brownrigg's puritan party, but he had shifted his position considerably since then, though he always remained a moderate man. In 1625 he had by royal mandate been given two years' leave of absence on full pay while chaplain to the ambassador at Paris, and he was already in 1630 a chaplain to King Charles. Richard Crashawe, who was admitted at Pembroke in 1632, praises Lany for his beautifying of the College chapel and his adding dignity to the services. John Tournay, Crashawe's tutor, was stopped from taking his B.D. degree for the High Church opinions which he had expressed in his degree sermon, and finally received the degree by royal mandate. In a private report made to Laud on the general state of discipline in the College chapels in Cambridge it is stated that at Pembroke "they endeavour for order, and have brought it to some good pass". Unfortunately the example set by Wren in the keeping of the College records was not maintained, and under Lany's Mastership the Admission Book was carelessly kept and no College order or decrees were entered in the Register. From the accounts it is possible to trace some considerable building in 1634, to which year the panelling in the old Hall belongs; probably the large bow-windowed wing of the Master's lodge dates from this time, but even the accounts during this period are less informative than usual.

During the thirty-six years between the election of Harsnett to the Mastership and the outbreak of the Civil Wars the average number of admissions to the College increased considerably and the names of some seven hundred members of the College can be traced. Divines naturally still predominate, and though the College under Beale and Lany had become royalist and Laudian, the divines are not all on one side. Of royalists Balcanquhall had become Dean of Durham and was to die while in flight from Parliamentary troops. Parliament ordered the books of Poclynton to be burnt: and John Hewitt was beheaded in 1658 for a plot against the Commonwealth. Samuel Puleyn survived the war and became Archbishop of Tuam. Of Fellows under Lany, who were to suffer for their views but afterwards were restored, Robert Mapletoft and Mark Frank became Masters of Pembroke, and Edmund Boldero, Master of Jesus. Ralph Brownrigg, who had left Pembroke soon after Beale's election, became Master of St Catharine's and Bishop of Exeter, and for all his leaning towards puritanism suffered persecution during the Commonwealth. William Fenner, one of the puritans who had been in opposition to Beale, incurred the disfavour of the Court. Edmund Calamy, a "tanquam" Fellow, became more famous as a prominent puritan, and still more famous was Roger Williams, a Watts scholar from Charterhouse, who flying from the persecution of Laud, founded the colony of Rhode Island. In other spheres of life, too, men who had been at Pembroke during these thirty-six years were found in both camps when war broke out. Thomas Lucas died defending Colchester against the Parliamentary forces and Jacob Preston was with King Charles during the last weeks of his captivity, while among the judges who condemned him to death were Cornelius Holland and William Heveningham. John Pettus served as governor of the Royal mines under Charles, and was an active royalist. Negligence in the keeping of the Admission Book makes it uncertain whether the College has any claim to two other distinguished royalists, Richard Bulstrode, the diplomatist, and Philip Warwick, the courtier historian.

Of the poets bred in the College during these years all were royalists. The greatest, Richard Crashawe, migrated after taking his B.A. to Peterhouse, where he became a Fellow. Ejected at the beginning of the war, he went abroad and joined the Roman Church. Thomas Stanley, a Fellow-Commoner, is perhaps better known for his edition of Aeschylus and his *History of Philosophy* than for his poetry. Two minor poets were William Hammond, a kinsman of Stanley and an ejected Fellow, and John Collup, who like many other royalists turned during the Commonwealth to the study of medicine. John Anthony, son of Francis Anthony, managed to earn money by the sale of his father's patent medicine without incurring the anger of the College of Physicians; he also wrote devotional books. John Pordage was an astrologer. A doctor of real importance who made a substantial contribution to the growing medical science of the period was Thomas Wharton, first of a family that was to send men to the College for two centuries. Among other scientists were Henry Coggeshall, who invented a slide-rule, and William Holder, who taught a deaf-mute to speak.

The lawyers like the poets were mostly royalist, John Temple was Speaker of the Irish parliament after the Restoration, and Chaloner Chute Speaker of the House of Commons in 1659. John Fountain was imprisoned by Parliament; Robert Baldock was to be counsel for the Crown against the Seven Bishops.

It was from a lawyer that the College received the greatest benefaction of the first half of the seventeenth century. Robert Hitcham had been a pensioner at the College in 1587 and had a distinguished legal career. In 1637, on the advice of Matthew Wren, wishing to benefit the College, he bought from the Earl of Suffolk the castle, manor and advowson of Framlingham in Suffolk and left them by will to the College, at the same time making the College trustees for other charitable bequests which he had planned. Besides this benefaction and that of Lancelot Andrewes there were others during these thirty-six years. Gregory Downhall's gift has been mentioned. Mrs Amy Livesey in 1617 bequeathed a rent-charge at Tooting Bec to found an exhibition, which was augmented in 1631 by her son-in-law, John Hobbs, and in 1639 the College came into a reversion under the will of Thomas James of a tenement in London, known as The Black Boy on Old Change, for the endowment of an additional Greek scholar.

The validity of Robert Hitcham's great bequest was still in doubt when the Civil War began. Lany's position as a chaplain of the king and the generally royalist outlook of the Fellows soon involved the College in the disturbances of the realm. In July 1642 John Pooley, a Fellow, who had been elected by royal mandate, was acting as the king's agent in the collection of money and plate for the royal war-chest. It must have been at this time that the College sent its plate to Charles, "for better safeguard", retaining only the cup which they believed to be the Foundress's cup and Thomas Langton's Anathema cup with its curse on any who gave it away, and some small pieces for ordinary use.[1] Already Matthew Wren, now Bishop of Ely, had been arrested and sent to the Tower, and the College in the ill-fortune which now befell one to whom they looked with pride and gratitude wrote him a letter of rather ominous comfort, reminding him of the Pembroke martyrs under Queen Mary, "Memineris Ridleium Bradfordiumque utrumque Pembrochianum". It seems probable that their sympathy took a more practical turn than mere letters of condolence, for at this date or at some subsequent time they seem to have conveyed to him the money in the chest of Lyndwode and Pyke. Mark Frank, in 1642 Treasurer of the College, and one of Wren's chaplains, had himself already fallen into disrepute with Parliament for a royalist sermon. In the autumn of this year the most fervent royalists among the Fellows seem to have already left Cambridge, and on December 26 William Dowsing, the Parliamentary Commissioner, visited the College and found only a few Fellows left. With these and Edmund Boldero he argued about the ornaments and pictures in the chapel, and finally, he states, he "broke ten cherubims, broke and pulled down 80 superstitious pictures". Parliamentary troops

---

[1] "Mr Minories' plate" of the early eighteenth century inventories was the piece of plate presented by Sigismund Meienreis, admitted Fellow-Commoner in 1614.

were already occupying Cambridge, and Pembroke suffered from the invasion of "multitudes of Common Soldiers who made of the Colleges meere Spittles and Bawdy-houses for rich and debauched Souldiers, being filled with Queans, Drabs, Fiddlers, and Revels night and day", and "when their ragged Regiments which had lyen lowzing before *Crowland* nigh a fortnight, were commanded to *Cambridge*, forthwith the Colleges were appointed for their Kennels, and fourscore were turned loose into one of the least Halls in the University [note in margin 'Pembr. Hall.'], and charged by their Officers to shift for themselves, who without any more ado, broke open the Fellows and Scholars Chambers, and took their Beds from under them."

In March 1644 Lany and most of the Fellows were ejected for "offending the privileges of Parliament and other scandalous acts in the University of Cambridge" and almost for a year the College was without a Head, and almost without Fellows and scholars, and those who were left "had not so much a College as an inn", and "this most ancient Refuge of the Muses passed into the Power of the Barbarous Soldiery".

On January 10, 1645, the Earl of Manchester, the Parliamentary Commander in East Anglia, put in a new Master, Richard Vines, formerly of Magdalene College, who had been a schoolmaster and was now a prominent Presbyterian divine. He and Lany a few months later met as antagonists at the abortive conference at Uxbridge, and he was to be one of the Presbyterians appointed by Parliament to attend Charles in his captivity. At the same time a number of Fellows were also intruded in the same way, their qualifications being vouched for by the Assembly of Divines sitting at Westminster. Vines seems to have made every effort to set the College going once more, and he chose as his chief lieutenant one of the new Fellows, William Moses, who had been a Watts Greek scholar from Christ's Hospital. In 1646 Moses was appointed College Registrary, and he set himself to start again the College Register, inaugurated by Wren but allowed to lapse since the death of Jerome Beale. Something of the moderate outlook of Moses, and probably of Vines and the rest of the new Society, is to be seen in the preamble which Moses composed giving an account of the interregnum, in which he goes out of

Ob. Aug. 15. An. Dom. 1636. Ætat. 64

SIR ROBERT HITCHAM

his way to pay a compliment to Matthew Wren's "historiola" of the Masters and Fellows, and adds, "atque utinam aliquis illius viri optime de Collegio meriti aemulus inveniatur". And indeed the Register gives proof that for the next fifteen years until the Restoration, largely it would seem by the guidance of Moses, the new Society did all it could to preserve the old traditions of the House. They were not, any more than their predecessors, without the troubles of faction; in the autumn of 1646 one of the junior Fellows, Ambrose Staveley, anticipated the "Pem", and produced a libellous pamphlet about his colleagues, called "Mercurius Valentius". The pamphlet is unfortunately lost, but it caused a terrible stir among the Fellows of Valence Marie, "Collegium denuo totum in fermento, fremere socios et frendere". Staveley, finally detected, was expelled. More serious was the second purge of the Society which followed upon Parliament's requiring an oath of obedience to the Commonwealth after the execution of the king. Among those who could not comply and were consequently expelled were Vines the Master, and one of the Fellows, Edward Stearn, who had survived the purge of the Earl of Manchester, but now departing scratched upon the window of his rooms, the first-floor rooms on the left-hand side as you come out of the screens into Ivy Court, a farewell message which survived undestroyed well into the eighteenth century:

> Longum floreas
> Grandæva Mater Pembrochiana
> Invidiæ Odiisq; Superstes!
> Hoc tibi ex Animo precatur,
> Immerens immerito
> Ejectus Filius. E.S. Oct. 29. 1650.

Some years after there is a tribute to Stearn's love of the place, in the entry in the Buttery Books, while he was still an ejected Fellow, of expense "for exceeding when Mr Stearn came in". Stearn was to survive till the Restoration and to return to his old rooms, but Vines died in 1656.

The new Master put in by Parliament was one Sidrach Simpson, "the great Independent". Simpson was still more of an absentee than Vines had been, being engaged in London on the Synod of

Westminster, but with the help of Moses he obtained from Cromwell an ordinance settling the long dispute about Sir Robert Hitcham's will in favour of the College.

He did not hold the Mastership for long, and on his death in 1655 the Fellows did not wait for any outside interference, but elected William Moses as his successor. Cromwell was angry, having already earmarked the office for someone else, but he yielded to the representations made by the Fellows of what they already owed to Moses's ability and energy.

William Moses possessed qualities which might have made him one of the greatest Masters of the College. Vines, who was reputed to know men as well as books, had recognised the outstanding qualities of this junior Fellow, and while Moses was still a B.A. often employed him upon important College business, especially entrusting to him the tuition of the scholars. Moses watched over the interest of his pupils so closely that it became a college proverb that success was certain "sub dispensatione Mosaica".

On election as Master, after settling the affairs at Framlingham, he threw himself into the urgent necessity of repairing the College buildings and adopted the modern expedient of launching an appeal for subscriptions, which he had printed in three forms, one in English, and two in Latin, and from certain variations between the two Latin appeals it is clear that they are aimed at the purses of the two main contending parties at the moment. Through Calamy he succeeded in obtaining the support of certain City Companies.

He also began the building of a new range of chambers, parallel to Harsnett's new building, on the south side of New Court, employing as architect one Peter Mills of London, bricklayer and citizen, a tenant of the College, and later to be one of the Surveyors of the City of London and associated with Christopher Wren in his rebuilding of the City after the Great Fire.

Of Fellows and Scholars under the intruded Masters, John Stone was the first American elected to a Fellowship; another American Fellow was John Haynes, who after the Restoration sent in his resignation, but it was "not accepted by reason of ye ill penning". William and Henry Sampson were a pair of able brothers, of whom Henry was one of Moses's most active lieutenants and William a great financial reformer after the Restoration: Thomas Maule went off to preach the gospel in Cornwall, with such success that he never returned to College, but probably to him may be attributed that invasion from Cornwall which was to become one of the outstanding features of the College admissions for nearly a century. The first of the Cornish host was Nathaniel Coga, admitted in 1653, Fellow in 1658, and afterwards Master. Of a number of puritan divines John Gosnall, the anabaptist, from Charterhouse, Thomas Doolittle and Samuel Clarke were to become the most famous. Nehemiah Grew, afterwards Secretary of the Royal Society, was one of the greatest of early English botanists.

In 1660 Benjamin Lany and such of the ejected Fellows as were alive and not disqualified by marriage or some other cause were restored to their Fellowships, and a certain number of the intruded Fellows were in their turn ejected. A few of those who had been elected during Moses's Mastership were confirmed by royal mandate, such as Clifford, Henry Sampson and Coga. Sampson never seems quite to have accepted the validity of Coga's election, and voiced his doubts from time to time during the following years. William Moses left the College and applied himself to the law with considerable success, becoming counsel to the East India Company. On his ejection from the Mastership, there were some legal difficulties in adjusting financial claims between him and the College, but he retained his good will towards Pembroke, and when he died, famous and rich, he left a large legacy to the College for general purposes and for scholarships from his old school, Christ's Hospital, thus establishing a connection to which the College was to owe among many worthy alumni such distinguished men as Sir Edward Thornton, Bishop Middleton, Thomas Barnes and William Haig Brown and two great Masters in James Brown and C. E. Searle. William Moses was buried in the new chapel, but there is no memorial of any kind over his grave.

After the Restoration there was a series of rapid changes in the Mastership. Lany was in 1660 rewarded for his sufferings on behalf of the royal cause by elevation to the see of Peterborough, but he retained his Mastership until 1662. In 1663 he was promoted to the see of Lincoln, and in 1667 he succeeded Wren at Ely. Dying in 1675 he left £350 to endow a bye-fellowship at the College and to augment the value of the Smart Fellowship with which he himself had entered the College in 1616.

Mark Frank, who followed him as Master, lived for only a year after his election. He was a good scholar, and left a large collection of books to the College library. He too had been rewarded for his loyalty to the king by preferment, and was Treasurer of St Paul's Cathedral, where he was buried.

The great event of these years was the building of the new chapel. Wren on his release from the Tower executed a vow that he had made during his long imprisonment. He had preserved the money of Lyndewode and Pyke's chest, which he now augmented to a hundred pounds. He also at his own cost built a new chapel for the College and endowed it with the manor of Hardwick to keep it in repair. For this building he employed his nephew Christopher, whose first work as an architect it was.

The chapel was consecrated in 1665. This addition to the College buildings had left an untidy mess between it and the south wing of the Old Court, with the Master's lodge huddling up against the Hostel. There was some idea of rebuilding the Hostel along the street front between the College and the chapel, and Frank in his will left money to help this project, but in 1664 the Fellows decided to build cloisters with chambers over them as a suitable link between the Old Court and the new chapel, and to pull down the Hostel.

Hitcham's will, like other lawyers' wills drawn by themselves, was most obscure and seemed to tie up his benefaction in such a way that the College could make no use of it, but Wren as the supervisor of the will, and the only man surviving who could have known the testator's intention, gave an interpretation of the will which enabled the College to make use of the income from their new property for new buildings provided that those buildings should bear the name of Hitcham. In 1667 Sir Robert Hitcham's cloisters were consecrated by Wren. In the same way the name of Hitcham was attached to the building which Moses had begun

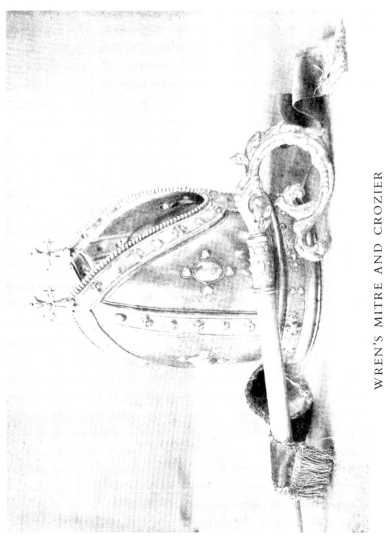

WREN'S MITRE AND CROZIER

to build with funds from the Framlingham property, and on both buildings his arms were properly displayed.

Wren himself died the following year, and on May 11 he was buried in the chapel after an elaborate ceremony devised for the funeral by his friend, William Dugdale the Herald. A silver mitre and crozier, carried in this procession and laid up in the chapel, are still in the possession of the College. Wren also left to the College the communion plate of his private chapel.

On Mark Frank's death the College elected as Master Robert Mapletoft, a chaplain and friend of Wren, who had been one of the ejected Fellows of 1642. He had been nominated for the Mastership when Lany resigned but had stood aside in favour of Frank. In 1667 he became Dean of Ely. Under him the buildings of the College were still further extended. The front near the chapel and the street was tidied up, the old gate of the Master's stables being removed, "it being as it is now an eye sore to the chapel". A fresh and more favourable lease of the *venella* was obtained from the town, over which Hitcham's building had already been encroaching, for a nominal rent and an annual sermon to be preached before the Mayor; and in 1670, chiefly through the generosity of two senior Fellows, William Quarles and Richard Ball, the north wing of this court was extended to its present length. In 1673 £2. 0s. 6d. was expended on the lime trees which flourished till the other day. For a short while too, about this time, the Fellows seem to have taken over as a "large parlour" one of the rooms in Hitcham's building looking over the New Court with its young trees and the stream crossed by three bridges running across it. In 1675 an organ built by Mr Thamar was added to the chapel.

For all this development careful economy was needed, and the active man of the moment was William Sampson. The Treasurer's accounts for 1667–8 record his "journey to London to agree with Coll: Tenants for rebuilding our Houses burnt by ye late fire". In the same year he established a new method of keeping the College accounts which was to remain unaltered for over a hundred and fifty years. He compiled a new lease Register, and generally reorganised the finances of the College. In 1672 Mapletoft appointed him President, but in 1675, after one final protest against the illegality of Coga's Fellowship, a protest which Coga refused to answer as the matter had already been settled, he went off to a country living at Clayworth in Nottinghamshire.

Mapletoft himself seems to have been a moderate and generous man, but of some stubbornness. Between 1668 and 1671 several attempts were made to intrude one Wormley Martin of Jesus into a Fellowship by royal mandate. Wormley Martin had the support of Edmund Boldero, the Master of Jesus, who told the Secretary of State that he knew there was no truth in the customary answer of the Fellows of Pembroke that all their Fellowships were full, and that there were pre-elected Fellows waiting "for profits". As a matter of fact Boldero was right, since one of William Sampson's methods of meeting the heavy expenses of repairs was to reserve the profits of one Fellowship for this purpose. Mapletoft, however, adopted a policy of going off to his deanery at Ely for six months, and not replying to the various letters sent to him on Martin's behalf, and Boldero was reduced to complaining, "I know the Dean's temper and intentions so well that I am of opinion that another mandamus must be sent and that a peremptory one". Martin however never got his Fellowship.

On August 20, 1677, at two in the morning Mapletoft died in College. Two hours later the Fellows met and elected as his successor Nathaniel Coga, whom they then admitted Master at six o'clock the same morning. This haste was not so indecent as it appears. When Mapletoft fell seriously ill, the Fellows had reason to expect a mandate to elect some Court favourite, and they had already tried to sound the Chancellor, Monmouth, and to win his support in resisting an infringement of their statutory right of free election. But they took no risks, and four hours after Mapletoft's death Coga was installed in his place. Mapletoft left to the College an estate at Coveney, from the income of which the College established anew the office of Catechist and two exhibitions.

Coga was master for sixteen years, during which the College finally assumed the shape which it was to retain unaltered for the whole of the eighteenth and almost half of the nineteenth century, and which is preserved in David Loggan's engraving made during the year of Coga's Vice-Chancellorship, 1681-2, except for one

THE COLLEGE AT THE END OF THE SEVENTEENTH CENTURY

further alteration—the conversion of the old chapel into a library. The beautiful plaster ceiling, which bears the date of 1690, can, since Henry Doogood, a London plasterer often employed by Christopher Wren, was paid for working upon it, be attributed to that great architect, whose son came into residence as a Fellow-Commoner in 1691. The work on the new library was chiefly paid for by private subscription, William Sampson from Clayworth, his brother Henry, and William Holder being among the chief benefactors. The development of the library had been for the last twenty years an object of College policy, and there had been considerable bequests of books, including Mark Frank's and Philip Bacon's; William Quarles, who died in 1672, left in addition to his books £100 to increase the stipend of the Librarian: "My desire being to helpe to maintaine a student Graduate in the University till he be Master of Arts, and that he be not forced to run hence in the country to teach others, before he hath been taught himself."

During the last forty years of the seventeenth century, after some revival at the Restoration, there was a steady decline in the average number of admissions. Among the Fellows elected during this period there were men who maintained the traditions of the College, and some of them were to form the nucleus of a rather remarkable Society during the early years of the eighteenth century. It cannot, however, be claimed that many distinguished men were bred in Pembroke Hall under Frank, Mapletoft and Coga. Thomas Richardson became Master of Peterhouse, and an elder statesman in the University whose advice was often sought. William Burkitt distinguished himself as a biblical scholar. John Fryer, who joined the College from Trinity, was a famous traveller and oriental scholar. That the Society was not without its distinction or attractions during this period is shown by two unusual admissions. In 1676 Thomas Sydenham, the great physician, who had entered his son for the College, put his own name on the College Books in order to take the M.D. degree. In 1684, during a visitation of Cambridgeshire, Gregory King, the herald and economist, joined the College as a Fellow-Commoner. The days, however, when Pembroke could be called "Collegium Episcopale" were gone. From Lany's death in 1675, if we exclude Thomas Wagstaffe, suffragan Bishop of Norwich from 1694 to 1712, and Joseph Henshaw of Magdalen Hall, Oxford, Bishop of Peterborough from 1663 to 1678, whose only connection with the College was that he took his M.A. by incorporation from Pembroke, only one Pembroke man for a hundred years reached episcopal dignity, William Cotterell, and he only held an Irish bishopric for less than a year.

CHAPTER V

THE EIGHTEENTH CENTURY

When Nathaniel Coga died the minds of the Fellows turned to his old antagonist, William Sampson, and two of them, Mark Anthony and Marmaduke Tyrwhitt, were despatched to Clayworth to inform him of his election. But Sampson had settled down to the life of a parson farmer, and the result of their journey is best told in the words of his diary.

1693. Dec. 24   Geo Norton's wife Buryed being Sunday & ye Sunday after George himself.

Dec. 28   Entertained Parishioners.

[1694] Jan. 18   Mr Anthony & Mr Tyrwhit two of ye Fells of Pemb Hall in Cambr. (upon ye death of Dr Coga) brought me Letters of my being Elected to ye Mastership of ye College. But I excused myself to ym.

Feb.   We headed 2 Rows of Willows in Parson Hern, being ye 1st fruites o' my Plantg.

Mar. 1st   We plow'd a peece o' my Orchyard & sow'd Beans wch did very well.

Accidents this year: A Cow drown'd in my Pond, a Foal overlaid by her Dam in ye Stables, & a Cow shot her Calf in ye Stanracks.

There in his rustic contentment Sampson remained, the only Master as far as records go who refused office after he had been elected. When he died in 1703 he bequeathed to the College the advowson of Earl Stonham in Suffolk.

The Fellows next thought of Thomas Browne, who had been in residence as an active Fellow until his presentation to Orton Waterville seven years before. Coga had been a chaplain of Matthew Wren, as Wren had been of Andrewes; Sampson, though he finally settled down as a country clergyman, had been elected to his Fellowship during the Commonwealth, and had a brother who never abandoned his puritanism; Browne did not matriculate till after the Restoration, and with him begins a new phase in the history of the College. It is significant that both Sampson and Browne were country parsons and not high ecclesiastical dignitaries.

Browne, who had married on going to Orton, retained the living with the Mastership. It was not possible for the Master, especially if he had a family, to live as he should on the Mastership alone, and as he was the first married man with a family for some time to occupy the Master's lodging, substantial repairs to it, especially in the kitchen, were carried out. His Mastership was a period of quiet consolidation. Numbers remained small, but an active and friendly body of Fellows was being formed, and there was plenty of domestic business to occupy them. The first act of Browne's Mastership was the transfer of the books from Booth's old library over the hall to their new home in the old chapel, a task entrusted to Anthony, Banckes and the junior Fellow, "Sir" Crossinge. By 1697 the work was done and new catalogues completed, and a charge in the accounts for "Strong beer and pipes in the Library" suggests some opening ceremony. The treasury was repaired and painted and Mr Webb, the attorney, was paid a guinea a year for assisting Richard Atwood "in perusing the writings &c in ye Treasury". The Master and John Westfield the tutor undertook to revise and bring up to date the Benefactors' Book, and Westfield was despatched to London to bargain with Dr Sherton for an original portrait of Archbishop Grindal which, with carriage, cost the College £7. 16s. 6d., and now hangs in the hall. The music in chapel was also the care of the Master, President Crouch and Westfield, who decided that the "preture" for the Organist must be increased. A *preture* was a levy on every member of the College whose name was on the boards, according to his standing in the House, i.e. Fellow, Fellow-Commoner, pensioner or sizar, for some specific service. The *preture* for the Organist was now raised so as "to ascertain a revenue of twenty pounds", on condition that he should instruct the Scholars "in singing as far as to enable them to chant the psalms in tune to ye Organ", and also those who were responsible for taking the services "in a tunable way of chanting them according to ye capacity of their voices". For this purpose the Organist, Thomas Tudway, Organist also of King's College, undertook to attend every Saturday between three and four. Unfortunately Tudway had a habit of making puns, and in consequence of one of these on July 29, 1706, the College Register records that "being proved guilty of speaking words highly reflecting upon her Majesty and government" he was deprived of his Organist's place. In March of the following year he was restored, and perhaps it was by his persuasion that in the same year the College entered into a bargain with Mr Charles Quarles for a new organ, the old one being taken down and set up in the church at Framlingham. Quarles's organ fell into disuse in 1778. When it was restored in 1863 the words "Bernard Smith fecit" were found inside one of the pipes and it is probable that though Quarles constructed the organ, the pipes came from the famous Father Smith.

Tudway's misfortune was not the only echo of political feeling which disturbed the tranquil reign of Thomas Browne. In a Society Jacobite in sentiment there was one Whig, Robert Lloyd. While he was Bursar one of his duties was to collect and pay the *preture* for the "town music", or waits, but in March 1697 he entered in his book:

In perpetuam Rei Memoriam Ego Robertus Lloyd Bursarius ob seditiosum cantum (viz. The King shall enjoy his own again) Musicis Preturam denegavi, subduxi, et ob eundem repetitum cantum penitus obliteravi.

His successor as Bursar was Richard Crossinge, who restored the *preture* and paid the arrears. Political events also deprived the College in 1702 of the services of John Westfield, the tutor, who refused to take the oaths required on the accession of Queen Anne, and in consequence of his non-juring lost his Fellowship. The College so respected his conscience "scrupulosa viri integerrimi mens", that he was made an allowance of ten pounds a year "in consideration of ye straightening of his circumstances upon the loss of his fellowship".

Browne died early in 1707 and Edward Lany succeeded. He was a great-nephew of Benjamin Lany, whose admirable portrait, now in the hall, he presented to the College, and he held the Bye-fellowship founded by his great-uncle. He had been a chaplain to William III, was Professor of Divinity at Gresham College and a Fellow of the Royal Society. He was also a man of affairs, and for a year or two the College had been employing him in their long tiresome litigation with the executors of Sergeant Moses. He was a strong Tory, and he came to preside over a College now, since Lloyd had lost his Fellowship through preferment by his patron the Duke of Bedford, entirely of one political colour. Lany's nickname in the University of "the blind horse" does not suggest acute powers of intrigue, but he was a very active politician. His "Mr Praeses" for most of his Master-ship was Reginald Hawkins, who was only prevented from being elected Vice-Chancellor by the intervention of Bentley, the great Master of Trinity, and between Bentley and Lany there seems to have been some sort of a feud. In 1716 Lany, to discredit Bentley by showing up how small his party was in the University, nominated him for a contested election to the Vice-Chancellorship. Bentley played up, appeared to rally his supporters, who however only put in an appearance at the Senate House to laugh the matter off and go away without voting, with the result that only two votes were given for Bentley as against 106 for his opponent. In the same year two of the Fellows of Pembroke, Richard Tyson, afterwards a famous physician, and John King, had held up a vote of congratulation to George I on the successful suppression of the Jacobite rising of 1715, but Bentley on this occasion successfully got round the opposition.

Lany also appears to have actively interested himself in the development of the College finances. In 1677, when Sampson was checking the library stock, there were counted out "one bag of half-crowns totalling £167, 1 bag of shillings totalling £140, another of shillings £33. 1. 0. and one of sixpences £22. 10. 0.", a total of 5797 silver coins: an unmanageable fund and of course lying idle.

Bishop Lany's £350 had for some years been lent on the security of a mortgage to another member of the family, but was also now lying idle. In 1707, just before Lany's election, there is an order that the President and Treasurers "shall with all convenient speed let out upon interest at good security", various moneys lying idle in the treasury, and from this time there begin to appear in the accounts references to loans to "the United Company trading to the East Indies", to a policy taken out with the Perpetual Assurance Office on behalf of the College ("the money to be received from the same office on the death of the member Thomas Brigby"), and to a "Lottery Bond of £420 principal in the lottery for raising £1,500,000 for the service of the year 1711". Bishop Lany's legacy passed through a series of conversions from the State lottery to bank annuities, and from bank annuities to what the Register records as a loan "Societati in mari Australi negotianti". But even before that bubble burst, the College had been trying "to fix" their uninvested money upon land, and with the money received from Sergeant Moses's estate for the exhibitions from Christ's Hospital farms were bought at Ashwell and at Milton. In all these financial trans-actions the Master was most active, being assisted by a former scholar of the College, Dr George Wharton, a member of a famous medical family.

The College was at this time in great need of well-organised finance, and evidence of financial stress is to be seen in a proposal to sell the impropriation of the Saxthorpe tithe. Expensive law-suits were pending, the most important concerning the livings of Sall and Cawston. In 1715 Erasmus Earle of Heydon in Norfolk, a former Fellow-Commoner, gave to the College the advowsons of these two parishes with certain conditions attached to the choice of incumbents. He died in 1721, having presented Edward Lany to Sall in the year before. Lany resigned in 1725, and Earle's sons contested the validity of their father's gift, and litigation between them and the College continued for six years. Another heavy expense was necessitated by the state of the buildings of Old Court, which it was wisely decided to ashlar. To this the College applied in 1712 a legacy of £50 from William Banckes the tutor, and a loan from Richard Atwood of £150 in 1716, and in 1718 the Master and all the Fellows agreed to give up the greater part of their dividends for the same purpose. And indeed Edward Lany had gathered under him a remarkably happy and united Society. In 1714 Francis Mundy, one of the Fellows, having married, resigned his Fellowship, "now I am become possess'd of the only Fellowship in the World preferable to that you bestowed on me", and concludes his letter with the wish "that Learning, good Humor & Pleasant Conversation may flourish at Pembroke Hall", and among those who helped to see Mundy's wish fulfilled were Reginald Hawkins, President from 1708 until he went to Soham in 1719; Christopher Selby, who was the chief Tutor from 1711 to 1729 and whose brother was College Butler; Thomas Ashburner, who came from St Bees and held the Grindal Fellowship; and a remarkable trio, Richard Atwood, James Jeffrey and Richard Crossinge.

Atwood held few or no College offices, but he was appointed to keep the College Register in Latin, and he brought up to date Matthew Wren's catalogue of Masters and Fellows, busied himself with the muniments, and assisted Robert Hawes, Steward of the College Manor of Framlingham, in writing the two chapters on the College, in his manuscript History of Framlingham, which, revised and augmented in 1798 by Robert Loder, have been for many years the only printed history of the College. The Fellows liked Hawes's book so well that they presented him with a silver cup, which the Master went to London to buy. Atwood was also one of the three Esquire Bedells of the University, and was renowned for his wit and for his Latin verses. His friend Crossinge described him, in his epitaph, as "Vir doctus, beneficus, pius, in rebus ludicris egregie fuit lepidus et elegans", and there is a zest about Atwood's minutes of College meetings which preserves some of his style, as when for the humble bedmakers' helps he invents the imposing title of "servulae vetulis lectisterniatricibus". Crossinge in the epitaph also refers to his love of fishing; among his effects sold after his death was a gun, and the neatest of his Latin poems is one entitled "To my puppy killed with my own hand". He presented to the College to adorn the library the portraits of Ridley, Bradford, Felton and Brownrigg which now hang in the hall. James Jeffrey was one of the Cornishmen and filled in his time almost all the College offices. Crossinge in his account book refers to him as Jeff, and from 1709 to 1735 they lived opposite each other in rooms over the present buttery, "the middle chambers on the left and right on the way up to the

Wilderness ", the Wilderness being what is now called the Rabbit-warren.

Crossinge came of a merchant family in Devonshire, and of all the Fellows of his time he seems to have been the one who most wholly identified himself with the College; from 1700 to 1735 he was never absent from the College for more than three or four days in any year, and almost all these absences were caused by his annual journey to Framlingham to hold the manorial court there on behalf of the College. A testimony to the love these men bore the College is to be found not only in the benefactions which they themselves made, but in the benefactions which the College received during the years which followed from men who had been in the College under them. Charles Parkin, Charles Stuart, and William Simon Warren all founded scholarships, Erasmus Earle gave the College two livings, Robert Trefusis panelled the parlour, and Wrightson Mundy paved the cloisters. Thomas Ralph, a Fellow, left £500 to the College, and another Fellow, James Brookes, left £100. Richard Frame, a former pensioner, bequeathed to the College in 1718 the sum of two hundred pounds, which the College in 1738 applied through Queen Anne's Bounty to the raising of the value of the living of Saxthorpe. Plate still in the possession of the College preserves the memory of the Fellow-Commoners of this period, and some of the finest pieces were chosen by Lany himself, as for instance Sir William Barker's basin and Richard Belward's ewer, gifts of two Jacobites which are still in use at the high table.

During the twenty-five years of Browne's and Lany's Masterships the entry was small, averaging about ten a year, but the material was good. Of three hundred and fifty-nine admitted members, fifty-three were from Cornwall. Two future Masters, John Hawkins and Roger Long, and a number of prominent Fellows, Richard Atwood, James Jeffrey, Francis Mundy, William Trollope, belong to these years. The College continued to attract men from other Colleges and other Universities; John Woodward, the geologist, founder of the Professorship which bears his name, took his M.D. from Pembroke in 1695, and Richard Tyson incorporated from Oxford and, after holding the Lany Fellowship for a short while, established himself in practice as a doctor in

London and was President of the College of Physicians. Of the physicians bred in Pembroke during these years, William Oliver, a Cornishman who settled in Bath and invented the Bath Oliver biscuit, is the most famous; Messenger Monsey, the eccentric physician of Chelsea Hospital, was the son of an old Pembroke scholar, Robert Monsey, the non-juror: George Wharton, who preserved the tradition of his family in the College, was Treasurer of the College of Physicians. John Whalley became Master of Peterhouse in succession to Thomas Richardson, also of Pembroke. Seawell Heatherly, one of the first Moses's exhibitioners from Christ's Hospital, returned to his old school to be headmaster of it. William Cotterell, for a short while Bishop of Ferns, was the only mid-eighteenth century bishop bred in the College. William Noll, whose sister had married Francis Mundy, became a judge of the High Court. Benjamin Keene was for a long while British ambassador at Madrid. William Shirley was Governor-General of Massachusetts.

Lany died in 1728, and with the College in debt owing to repairs and extensive lawsuits the Fellows felt the need of a rich, substantial man of affairs as his successor. They chose a former Fellow-Commoner, John Hawkins, Rector of Bradwell-juxta-Mare, whose father was reputed to have been the most wealthy lawyer Cornwall had ever produced. He was elected Master on August 15, 1728, and in November he came to the College, was admitted to his office, and then after a few weeks went back to Cornwall, and there he remained for the next two and a half years, Richard Crossinge as President governing in his stead. Every year Hawkins gave up the emolument of his office, which was applied to the debts of the embarrassed Treasury. In May 1731 he came up once more for a few weeks, and then went back to Cornwall, never to return to Cambridge. In 1733 he resigned his Mastership in a letter beginning:

When you did me the Honour of electing me Master of Pembroke-Hall I thought my affairs in the country would have given me leave to have visited you pretty often. But as I have found myself mistaken, I imagin'd I could not do better than by resigning my Mastership to put it in your Power to choose a

Successor of Superior Abilities, and one, who is more att leisure, than I am, to discharge the Trust you shall repose in him.

It had not been an ideal Mastership, but the four hundred and fifty pounds of his emoluments which Hawkins had surrendered had, with a hundred pounds from Lord Anglesey and two other gifts of fifty pounds, one from Dr Gascarth, a former Fellow, Rector of All Hallows, Barking, who left a number of books to the library, and the other from Mr John Hungerford of Lincoln's Inn, raised the Treasury from that penury which Richard Atwood's minutes had so often lamented.

Hawkins's successor, Roger Long, was one of the real "characters" of eighteenth-century Cambridge. Born at Croxton, north of Thetford, he lived, while at the King's School, Norwich, with his uncle Roger Howman, M.D., of Caius, a doctor practising in that city. Long had intended to take up "chirurgy", but Howman persuaded him to go up to Cambridge, and in 1697 he was admitted as a sizar at Pembroke. His commonplace book, preserved in the College library, in which he records a resolution to spend ten hours at his books daily, and his opinions of what he reads, with reflections on his own shortcomings, reveals a real passion for learning, but after taking his B.A. he was forced by family poverty to leave the "tranquil seat of the Muses", and take up work as a schoolmaster at the Grammar School at Soham. In a brief autobiography of his early life he records, as an omen that better things were in store for him, that once while riding he was thrown from his horse and lost his way in the fens, but managed to find himself on the road to Isleham. His faith in his own destiny was rewarded, and in 1703 he was elected to a Fellowship at Pembroke on the same day as Richard Atwood. In 1714 his "Music Speech" at Commencement won him a reputation as a wit, and in the following year the College employed him to compose the letter of thanks to Erasmus Earle. But he was soon again to drift away from Pembroke. In 1716 he was presented to the living of Orton Waterville, vacant by the death of Thomas Thomas, a former Treasurer and Bursar of the College, who had drowned himself while trying to shave by the reflection of his face in the rectory well. Long's letter resigning his Fellowship at the end of his year of grace is dated from Market Bosworth, where he had also taken up the duties of tutor in the family of Sir Wolstan Dixie. These duties brought him back to Cambridge, and he resided for some time at Emmanuel as a Fellow-Commoner. In 1728 he took his D.D. and returned into residence at Pembroke as a Fellow-Commoner. He had by this time distinguished himself as a lecturer on astronomy. He retained his living of Orton after his election as Master until 1751, when he was presented to Bradwell, Essex. He was also Vicar of Cherry Hinton. He was a man of great ingenuity. In the Fellows' garden he contrived a cold bath for which he himself constructed the engine, while on the "water work" in his own garden he contrived to paddle himself about upon a kind of water-velocipede. He also built a hollow revolving sphere or planetarium, re-presenting on its inner surface the apparent movements of the heavenly bodies.

He was in 1733 a vigorous active man of fifty, and in the year of his election the Tory vote carried him into the office of Vice-Chancellor. An attempt, however, to nominate him for the next year also was prevented by Bentley.

But the old company in the Pembroke parlour, to which Francis Mundy had paid so graceful a tribute, was passing away. Between 1731 and 1736 Reginald Hawkins, Atwood, Selby, Jeffrey, Crossinge and Ashburner all died. Jeffrey had in 1734 on the death of Selby been presented to the living of Framlingham, but his long partnership with Crossinge was not to end by his going there, where Crossinge's annual visit would have renewed their companionship, for in February 1735, while Jeffrey was still in residence during his year of grace and still Bursar, Richard Crossinge died, and a week later Jeffrey died also. Both were buried in the ante-chapel. Jeffrey left fifty pounds to the College for an annual sermon upon Good Friday, and Crossinge left almost all his estate to the College. Most of this consisted in mortgages on the houses between the chapel and the lodge of Peterhouse, and as the mortgages fell in the College acquired this addition to its site. On it stands now the Red Buildings, which, if it had any of the architectural grace of Crossinge's age, ought perhaps to be given his name; for an examination of the accounts

Rogerus Long S.T.P.

ROGER LONG

THE GREAT SPHERE IN 1871

(On the extreme left is John Power, Master (1870–1880); on the extreme right is Robert Plane, afterwards Porter of Lodge Court)

during the long period of his activity suggests his great efficiency, and that the College rode buoyantly over the difficulties of these years was in great measure due to Richard Crossinge, son of the Plymouth merchant.

In the year of Crossinge's death a Fellow was elected who was gradually during the next ten years to assume leadership in the Society. James Brown had been one of the earliest of the Moses exhibitioners from Christ's Hospital, and he was in the Grecian tradition of that school a humanist, and we can imagine not altogether in sympathy with "the more than mathematic gloom" of Cambridge studies at this time.

In 1743, owing to a tradition that the College was founded in 1343, a date which Wren had already refuted, but which was to stand as official until Ainslie altered it in the Calendar of 1840, the College celebrated its four hundredth anniversary. Thomas Gray, the poet, still at Peterhouse, but already on intimate terms of friendship with several of the Fellows of Pembroke, wrote to one of them, Wharton, whose family entered at Pembroke throughout the whole of the seventeenth and eighteenth centuries, "Wont you come to the Jubilee? Dr Long is to dance a Saraband & Hornpipe of his own Invention without lifting either Foot once from the ground." The Jubilee was held at the Foundress's Feast on January 1, 1743–4, and Christopher Smart, who had been admitted as a sizar in 1739, composed and probably recited a Secular Ode. He invokes Spenser, and repeats the legend of the death of the Foundress's husband upon her wedding day, though Atwood had already cast sufficient doubt on this legend for it to be removed from the Order of Commemoration:

> All that is great and good she now pursues;
> She meditates a mansion for the muse,
> Nor will she lose a day.

And he concludes:

> To Granta now, where gentle Camus laves
> The reedy shore, and rolls her silver waves,
> She flies, and executes, with bounteous hand,
> The work her mighty soul had plann'd
> And unborn minds she forms, and future souls she saves,

And to ensure that work to endless fame,
Left what can never die, her own illustrious name.
  Let others with enthusiasm fill'd,
  Nunneries and convents build;
Where decayed with fasts and years,
  Melancholy loves to dwell
  Moaping in her midnight cell,
And counts her beads, and mumbles oer th'unmeaning pray'rs.

Religious joys and sober pleasures,
Virtuous ease, and learned leisure,
Society and books, that give
Th'important lesson how to live:
These are gifts, are gifts divine,
For, fair Pembroke, these were thine.

Two years later the only substantial alteration to the buildings
between the completion of the new library in 1690 and the
disasters of 1876 was made when a new western front to the
Master's lodge was built for £84 according to the plans of
Mr Greaves, and on December 17, 1745, when the Young
Pretender was at Derby, the Society unanimously voted fifty
pounds for his majesty's service. But behind this appearance
of agreement trouble was stirring about the filling of vacant
Fellowships.

In the spring of 1746 an elaborate scheme of lectures was drawn
up in which the bias was clearly towards the humanities, and
Christopher Smart, now a Fellow, was assigned a substantial share
of the lecturing. Gray, who with Brown seems to have been in
sympathy with this lightening of the "more than mathematic
gloom", was pressing the claims of a friend of his own from
Peterhouse, Henry Tuthill, but at an election in October 1746
Roger Long, after the statutory three nominations had shown
Tuthill with a clear majority over his own candidate, Knowles
of Pembroke, exercised his power of veto, refused to allow an
election to go forward, and wrote in the Register, "Ego non
consentio". The Fellows had already been taking legal opinion
on the Master's powers, but Long was obstinate, threatening them
with a Visitor. What Gray writes of the atmosphere of the

Pembroke parlour shows it now a very different place from that which Mundy had enjoyed. "In short they are all as rude as may be, leave him at Table by himself, never go into Parlour, till he comes out; or if he enters, when they are there, continue sitting even in his own Magisterial Chair. May bickers with him publickly about twenty paltry Matters and Roger tother day told him he was impertinent."

This unhealthy state of affairs continued for three years. As it was very difficult to hold an election meeting except at the annual Audit, owing to the number of absentee Fellows, things were bound to move slowly. At the Audit of 1747 Long proposed to devote all the five Fellowships then vacant to the uses of the Treasury, but the Fellows forced him to proceed to an election to two of them, and put up a new candidate, William Mason, a clever Johnian with a reputation as a poet, with whom Gray had lately formed a friendship. He too was a humanist. He received the necessary voices at the nominations, but again the Master vetoed an election, writing in the Register:

Ego non consentio ut extraneus eligatur socius, cum domesticos habeamus idoneos, et dignos qui in ordinem sociorum co-optentur.

This was probably a false step, because although Long's desire not to discourage Pembroke scholars may have been laudable, the statutes gave the Society full freedom of choice from graduates of Oxford or Cambridge. At the same meeting with better justification Long refused to consent to the presentation of Bedford, one of the Fellows opposing him, to the living of Earl Stonham, because Bedford had told him that he proposed to ask the Bishop's permission to reside in Cornwall while he held the living.

For another year and a half this deadlock continued, until the persistence of the Fellows led by James Brown broke through the obstinacy of the Master, and in March 1749 Knowles, Tuthill and Mason were all three elected, and Gray writes in triumph of "The Peace of Pembroke signed between the high and mighty Prince Roger, surnamed the Long, Lord of the Great Zodiack, the Glass Uranium, and the Chariot that goes without Horses on the one Part, and the most noble James Brown, the most serene Theophilus Peele, and the most Profound Nehemiah May &c. on the other."[1] In April the treaty was confirmed by the Master's appointment of James Brown as his President.

In the years of discord Smart had got into trouble. In the spring of 1747 he had been in the heyday of extravagance, when he produced in the College hall his play, "The Ungrateful Fair, or A Trip to Cambridge", of which the prologue, a few songs and the soliloquy of the Princess Perriwinkle survive. Richard Forester, afterwards Fellow of Pembroke, acted the part of the heroine. Living in the expensive set of rooms which now forms the senior parlour he was running up large debts, and the Buttery Sizing Book shows a startling disproportion of *Potus* over *Panis*. Gray, concerned at this folly, wrote: "All this you see must lead to Jayl or Bedlam", and in November of the same year he was arrested for an old debt to a London tailor; from this he was freed by a subscription among his colleagues, but he was advised to "go off in the night" to avoid arrest. He returned to College in 1748 and lived for a year more quietly in other rooms over the buttery, but in November 1749 he left Cambridge for journalism in London, and in 1753 his Fellowship lapsed through his being "credibly reported to be married". He was allowed to keep his name on the College boards so that he might go on competing for the Seatonian Prize, which he had already won four times. In 1756 he went out of his mind and was confined until September 1762. In April 1763 his *Song to David* was published, and Mason wrote to Gray in June of that year: "I have seen his Song to David, and from thence conclude him as mad as ever." He died in a debtors' prison in 1771.

During Long's battle with the Fellows and for some years before the numbers of admissions had been dropping; in 1740 there had been so few scholars that sizars, Smart among them, had been paid for "performing the duties of Scholars in the house", and the quality of some of the entry had not been too good. In December 1746, after the opening of hostilities

---

[1] Peele was named "John" and May "Samuel". "Theophilus" and "Nehemiah" are facetious substitutes.

between Long and the Fellows the Master had taken as his own pupil a young Fellow-Commoner, John Blake Delaval, but almost immediately had had to send him down, for flaunting about Cambridge with a woman disguised as an officer of the army. After the peace had been concluded Gray wrote to Wharton:

I wish you would send them up some Boys, for they are grown extremely thin from their late long Indisposition....

and some months later he wrote again:

I have hopes that these two [i.e. Mason and Tuthill] with Brown's assistance, may bring Pembroke into some Esteem, but then there is no making Bricks without Straw. They have no Boys at all, and unless you can send us a Hamper or two out of the North to begin with, they will be like a few Rats straggling about an old deserted Mansion-House.

Gray's hopes were to some extent fulfilled; two years later he notes that the College "is picking up again; they have twelve admissions this year". The entry improved in quality as well as in number. Men of birth and wealth entered the College, William Taylor-How in 1751 and William Palgrave in 1753, both of whom later held bye-fellowships; and in 1754 Edward Southwell, who in 1776 succeeded to the Barony of Clifford. In 1755 the Earl of Strathmore was admitted as a Fellow-Commoner, and he was followed by two of his brothers, one of whom became a Fellow.

But though Mason probably played some part in getting these "Boys", neither he nor Tuthill was to remain long an active resident Fellow. Mason's reputation as a poet had secured for him the honour of composing the ode for the installation of Newcastle as Chancellor in 1749. In 1754 he was ordained and became Rector of Aston and Chaplain to the Earl of Holdernesse. In 1756 the Register had recorded the deprivation of Tuthill of his Fellowship for absence: "Since Mr Tuthill's absence fame has laid him under violent suspicion of having been guilty of great enormities, to clear himself of which he has not made his appearance and there is good reason to believe he never will."

Gray felt his friend's disgrace keenly, and no doubt all the more because a year before he had himself left Peterhouse and joined

Pembroke. There seems to be truth in the legend that certain gay young men in Peterhouse, knowing of his rope-ladder and his fear of fire, played a prank on him, and on March 6, 1756, he crossed the road and took up his residence in the College in which for many years before he had so many friends, finding himself "extremely well lodged here, and as quiet as in the Grande Chartreuse; everybody (even the Dr Longs and the Dr Mays) are as civil as they could be to Mary de Valence in person". His first quiet lodging was in the middle room over the western half of the junior parlour, but a year later he moved into the rooms over the senior parlour, where he lived till his death.[1]

Gray's position in Pembroke is clear from the fact that in 1757, when there was a rumour that Roger Long was dying, James Brown actually thought of proposing Gray for the Mastership, if he would qualify himself by taking orders. Gray, however, saw that there was only one proper successor to Long, and as soon as he heard the rumour began to move all the influence he could on behalf of Brown, soliciting Walpole with the assurance that Brown's "Principles in Government" were "those of every true and rational Whig", and sounding Mason on the views of the Fellows. But Gray was right when he added, "Dr Long,—if he is not dead, will recover, mind if he don't". He was right too in his choice of a man, for Long, who was still vigorous for his nigh eighty years, necessarily did less, and Brown was more and more in charge of College affairs. As early as 1750 he had shown determination as Proctor, "in the midst of Tumults and Mutinies", in enforcing the new University regulations for discipline, and controlling the Westminster Club. He was a small man: "He wants nothing but a foot in height and his own Hair, to make him a little old Roman," Gray wrote of him. He was short-sighted and precise in manner. Year in and year out he lived in College, "immersed in Livy and Quintilian". He had his own little garden, a strip walled off from the

[1] Curiously enough his fear of fire was to receive some justification in his new College; for in 1768 the other wing of Ivy Court was badly burnt, and he wrote: "I assure you it is not amusing to be waked between 2 and 3 in the morning, and to hear, 'Don't be frightened, Sir, but the College is all of a fire'."

THOMAS GRAY

Fellows' garden, and appropriated to the Senior Fellow. He played a game of bowls, and his pair of bowls, marked "J. B.", is still in use.

There was now in Pembroke something of the old amenity of the early years of the century. Christmas was a festive season; Gray talks of "the Copuses and Welsh Rabbets", and in October 1761 he wrote to Mason: "Here is Mr Dillival, and a charming set of Glasses that sing like nightingales, and we have concerts every other night." Mr "Dillival" was Edward Hussey Delaval, a younger brother of the unfortunate Mr Delaval mentioned above. He had been elected Fellow in 1751: he was a distinguished scholar and man of science, and he had made the completest set of musical glasses in England.

The Master would undoubtedly have enjoyed the concerts with Delaval's musical glasses. Cole notes of him that he "plays Harpsichord and Organ composes and even makes chimical operations".

Benefactions about this time included a hundred pounds from William Simon Warren in 1748 to provide an addition to the Holmes Scholarship from Blackrode Grammar School, and £500 in 1756 from Thomas Ralph for the Library and the augmentation of the Crossinge Fund.

In 1768 Gray was appointed Regius Professor of Modern History, but it was as a poet, and not as a historian, that in 1769 he gave further life to the legend, already as a result of Atwood's researches removed from the Benefactors' Book, that Aymer de Valence was killed upon his wedding day, when in his ode for the installation of the Duke of Grafton as Chancellor, he wrote of

Sad Chatillon on her bridal morn
Who wept her bleeding love.

To the last Roger Long maintained his vigour. In 1764 he had thrown himself into the contest for the High Stewardship of the University: "Dr Long, whose old Tory Notions that had long lain by and neglected, are brought out again and furbished for present use, tho' rusty and out of joint, like his own Spheres and Orreries."

He even in 1769 contemplated, though he was already eighty-nine, standing again for the office of Vice-Chancellor, but the University felt that he was too old, and though he was nominated, he was not elected.

It was in 1769 too that Benjamin Wilson painted the remarkable portrait of him which hangs in the College hall. On December 16, 1770, he died, and was buried in the vault under the chapel. The night was so windy "that the Flambeaux could scarcely be kept light", and the vault was found to be flooded, some said, because of the "uncommon wet season", but others thought the flooding was "occasioned by the waterworks" made by Dr Long "just at the head of the chapel where it oozed in". The antiquary Cole thought the funeral service not dignified enough—only the Fellow who read the prayers and the Scholar who read the lessons were in surplices—and "the Organ started up a sort of Solemn Voluntary without voices, as the corpse was brought into the Chapel, and finished the moment it was set down in the middle of it, and never played again". Cole witnessed the ceremony because he had called on Gray with a message from Walpole, but hearing that Gray was in the parlour with the Fellows, did not disturb him, but sent a note next day in which "in a jocose way I told him of the unceremonious and indecent manner of the Funeral", saying "they had brought the poor Mr from a warm Hall and noble Fire and flung him into a Well or ditch half full of Water". Gray's terse reply to this jocosity ran: "How did we know pray? Nobody here remembered another Burying of the Kind. shall be proud of your Advice on the next Opportunity which we hope will be some Forty years since." On which Cole comments: "It half looks as if the Society thought I was impertinent in taking notice of the slovenly manner of the Funeral. I was only in Jest." Long left to the College £400 of bank annuities and the unsold stock of his astronomy, which brought in £200, and another £200 of bank annuities to pay an exhibition to a scholar to look after the sphere and show it to visitors. His chief executor was Richard Dunthorn; a note in Long's hand in the Register records under the date of January 8, 1737-8, "My man Rd. Dunthorn came", and Dunthorn later became College Butler; the books kept in his beautiful handwriting are preserved in the treasury. He also compiled a set of astronomical tables. After Long's death he resigned the post of Butler, being succeeded by Gray's servant Stephen Hempstead. He is probably the only College Butler whose name is to be found in the *Dictionary of National Biography*.

During Long's thirty-five years' tenure of the Mastership the entry declined seriously, only 193 names being recorded during that period. For in spite of some recovery after the peace of 1749, the average for the last twelve years dropped to under four. Christopher Smart, in spite of his disturbed career, and Thomas Gray, the migrant from Peterhouse, are the chief glories of this attenuated band. Among the Fellow-Commoners E. H. Delaval and William Brabazon Ponsonby, who earned a considerable political reputation as a supporter of Fox, were the most famous. Edward Wilson was chaplain to the Earl of Chatham and private tutor to his son, while Joseph Turner, Senior Wrangler in 1767, and George Pretyman were to be his College tutors, and Pretyman was to break the long lack of bishops. Among minor worthies were Charles Jenner, who migrated to Sidney and wrote novels, and William Gibson, who won the Seatonian Prize; and divines such as Richard Baker, C. E. de Coetlogon and Paul Wright.[1]

On the evening of Long's funeral the Fellows elected James Brown Master. He was now just sixty-one, "small and short-sighted"; nine years later Cole noted that he was "as lively and active as a young man of 20: when I say lively I mean in Spirits and Activities: for his shortsightedness casts a gloom over his Countenance, which has too much of it without it". His politics had remained unchanged. An open letter to him in *The Cambridge Chronicle* of January 14, 1772, when he was Vice-Chancellor, signed 'Plain Truth' and supporting the agitation against the compulsory subscription to the thirty-nine articles, refers to his "known character for moderation". Four years after his election as Master, Thomas Plumer Byde put up as candidate for the Borough, chiefly supported by "the populace and low people", and even by dissenters, and Brown, so the old Tory Cole felt, "took an indecent Part in his Favour, as he was so supported, and Government unasked had 3 years before given him a good

[1] He was Rector of Shoreham and Vicar of Ugley, but he usually omitted his rectory from the title-pages of his publications.

living". The living which Brown had been given was that of Stretham, near Ely. Gray was naturally delighted with his friend's election and with his preferment; writing in February 1771 "the Old Lodge has got rid of all its harpsichords and begins to brighten up. its inhabitant is lost like a Mouse in an old cheese". But Gray was not long to enjoy his friend's success, for on July 30, 1771, he died in his rooms in College. In the year of his death William Mason presented to the College some chairs for the Master's lodge and a painting of Edmund Spenser, a copy made by Benjamin Wilson from an original now lost. In 1776 he and Brown each gave fifty pounds to start a building fund in memory of Gray, "not to be applied to any slight or accidental repairs of the College but to be put out to interest and increased till such time as the Society shall find it expedient to rebuild one whole side of either of the Quadrangles or a new building next the garden". Some years later another friend of Gray, Richard Stonhewer of Peterhouse, bequeathed to Pembroke a portrait of Mason by Joshua Reynolds, a painting of Gray done after his death by Benjamin Wilson and three of Gray's commonplace books, in which is contained one of the three autograph manuscripts of the famous Elegy. In 1810 the College arranged with T. J. Matthias to publish a selection from these books with an edition of Gray's Poems, but this act of piety was not profitable and the College presented a copy of the large paper edition to each Fellow on election. Soon after Brown became Master, after long and complicated litigation the bequest of Charles Parkin of over £5000 and of land at Barton-Bendish matured for the endowment of close scholarships from Merchant Taylors' School and from Bowes Grammar School in Yorkshire, and a year later the reversion of £1250 from Charles Stuart also fell in for another scholarship from Merchant Taylors'.

Under Brown, with Turner as Tutor, the College continued the prosperous career of revival which the last years of Roger Long's Mastership had witnessed. In 1772, 1780 and 1781 the College had the Senior Wrangler, George Pretyman, St John Priest, and Henry Ainslie of St Bees, the first of that family to come to Pembroke and father of Gilbert Ainslie, Master in 1828. Among other prizemen was B. E. Sparke, who with

Burton Pynsent, Oct.r 3:d 1773.

Sir

Apprehensions of gout, about this
Season, forbid my undertaking a journey
to Cambridge with my Son. I regret this
more particularly, as it deprives me of an
occasion of being introduced to your Personal
Acquaintance, and that of the Gentlemen
of your Society; a loss I shall much wish
to repair, at some other time. Mr Wilson,
whose admirable Instruction, and affectionate
Care have brought my Son, early, to
receive such farther advantages, as he can
                                            now

not fail to find, under your eye, will present Him to you. He is of a tender Age, and of a health, not yet firm enough to be indulged, to the full, in the strong desire he has, to acquire useful knowledge. an ingenuous mind and docility of temper will, I know, render him conformable to your Discipline, in all points. too young for the irregularities of a man, I trust, he will not, on the other hand, prove troublesome by the Puerile sallies of a Boy. such as he is, I am happy to place him at Pembroke; and I need not say, how much of his

Parents Hearts, goes along with him..
I am with great esteem and regard,

Sir

Your most faithful
and most obedient humble
servant
Chatham.

Pretyman was destined to break down the long bishopless record of the "collegium episcopale". Another distinguished cleric, John Gamble, came from Christ's Hospital; he became a Fellow and later achieved fame as an inventor of telegraphic signalling and the first Chaplain-General of the Forces.

The chief glory, however, of Brown's Mastership was the admission in 1773 of the young William Pitt. His private tutor from the age of nine and chaplain to Lord Chatham, Edward Wilson, persuaded Chatham to send his son to Pembroke, where Wilson's younger brother Thomas was a Fellow. Pitt was just under fifteen when he was admitted and had just turned that age when he came into residence, preceded by a letter from Chatham to Joseph Turner which is still in the possession of the College:

Sir,

Apprehension of gout, about this season, forbid my undertaking a journey to Cambridge with my Son. I regret this more particularly, as it deprives me of an occasion of being introduced to your Personal Acquaintance, and that of the Gentlemen of your Society, a loss I shall much wish to repair, at some other time. Mr Wilson, whose admirable Instruction, and affectionate Care have brought my Son, early to receive such further advantages, as he cannot fail to find under your eye, will present Him to you. He is of a tender Age, and of a health not yet firm enough to be indulged, to the full, in the strong desire he has to acquire useful knowledge. An ingenious mind and docility of temper will, I know, render him conformable to your Discipline, in all points. Too young for the irregularities of a man, I trust, he will not, on the other hand, prove troublesome by the Puerile sallies of a Boy. Such as he is I am happy to place him at Pembroke, and I need not say, how much of his Parents Hearts goes along with him.

I am with great esteem and regard,

Sir

your most faithful and most obedient humble Servant,

CHATHAM.

He was lodged in the rooms of the absent Thomas Wilson, the rooms in which Gray had lived, and found them neat and convenient, and Edward Wilson, who came up with him, remained in residence with him, although the direction of his studies was entrusted entirely to the two chief College Lecturers, Joseph Turner and George Pretyman, especially to Pretyman. But soon after his arrival the boy was taken seriously ill, and the old family nurse, Mrs Sparry, and Chatham's own physician, Dr Addington, hurried to Cambridge, to find him well looked after under the care of Dr Glyn. This is the origin of the legend, current from the early nineteenth century, that Pitt was so young when he came up that he was accompanied by his nurse. After his illness he was absent from Cambridge till the following summer, when he returned to College, and during the Long Vacation he was reading Cicero's *De Senectute* with James Brown in the lodge. It was not considered safe for him to stay in residence during the winter following, but when he returned in May 1775, no longer accompanied by Mr Wilson, he began to reside regularly for long periods during this and the four following years, changing his rooms in 1777, first to the Fellows' set over the buttery, and then to those at the eastern end of the north wing of Ivy Court. His studiousness was remarkable, and though he took his M.A. without any examination as "filius nobilis", it was only because his health had prevented him keeping the necessary terms. His friends in Pembroke were John Hamilton, afterwards Earl of Abercorn, Edward Eliot who married his sister, and Robert Wharton.

After his father's death in 1778 he resided less, but still came up for long periods until 1780, when he gave up his rooms in College and took chambers in Lincoln's Inn. In 1781 he entered Parliament, and in 1783 he became Prime Minister. In 1784 he was elected one of the University Burgesses and he continued to represent the University till his death, and it was in the same year that he presented to the College a handsome soup-tureen. In 1806 when Joseph Turner, for the second time Vice-Chancellor, was in London bearing an address of congratulation to the king on the victory at Trafalgar, he heard of the death of his former pupil. Pretyman, by that time Bishop of Lincoln, was with Pitt at the time of his death. In 1833 a bust of Pitt by Sir Francis

Chantrey was presented to the University by Lord Farnborough and placed in the hall of Pembroke, and the College possesses a posthumous portrait of him painted by G. H. Harlow in 1813 and one of him as a boy attributed to Gainsborough, as well as one of the busts made by Nollekens.

Brown died in 1784, leaving to the College over six hundred pounds. He was buried in the ante-chapel under a stone marked J. B. and Joseph Turner succeeded him as Master to hold the office for forty-four years, longer than any other Master in the history of the College. During the first twenty years of his Mastership the College undoubtedly maintained its record for scholarship, and continued to win a fair number of University distinctions. Among these prizemen were Edward Maltby, afterwards Bishop of Durham, and a group of able scholars from Christ's Hospital, of whom the chief were Edward Thornton, diplomatist and ambassador to the United States, A. W. Trollope, headmaster of Christ's Hospital, and Thomas Fanshawe Middleton, the first Bishop of Calcutta. The University was steadily reforming itself, and there is no doubt that the standard of scholarship was rising in the College. In 1790 College prizes were instituted of books stamped with the College Arms. Yet the old age was not yet passed, and in 1791 a purely personal quarrel resulted in the last fatal duel in Cambridge being fought between two Pembroke scholars, Henry Applewhaite and Richard Rycroft. Rycroft died of his wounds, and the grand jury at Bury threw out the bill of murder against Applewhaite. The College was not unaffected by the strain and stress of national affairs. In 1798 the Society voted £200 to assist the Government in carrying on the war, in 1813, £30 to relieve the Russians, in 1814, ten guineas to the sufferers at Leipzig, and in the same year ten guineas to the dinner to the poor of Cambridge in celebration of the peace. The economic effects of the war are to be seen in the growth of the value of tithe and in the increase of the price of provisions. The livings of Saxthorpe and Waresley, which had not been previously of sufficient value to entail the loss of Fellowship upon a Fellow who accepted them, were now by agreement put into that class, and in the same year (1800) a bonus was distributed among the College servants on account of the high price of provisions. In 1799 land at Sawston was sold to redeem the land tax on College estates. And after the war numbers of young men thronged to Cambridge, and in 1819 the College actually put into a tenantable state of repair attics over the old library above the hall, although the College was still so small that when in 1815, owing to a fever, the Easter term was allowed to undergraduates and the servants had to be compensated, there were only three bedmakers and one shoeblack.

Material benefactions continued to accrue to the College. In 1782 Mistress Mary Barker of Cambridge left the College a legacy of £600. Behind this benefaction lies a curious story. Samuel May, a Cornishman, who came up in 1733 and was elected a Fellow, was a Tutor from 1747 to 1776, and was appointed President by James Brown in 1770. Gray did not like him and he seems to have been an odd character. He had accumulated some wealth, and on several occasions lent money to the College. In February 1782 the living of Framlingham became vacant, and as May was senior Fellow, by tradition the offer of the living had to be made to him. But he was now sixty-seven, and he was also engaged to be married to Mistress Mary Barker, who was apparently old, illiterate, and without the sight of one eye. To marry her would have meant the loss of his Fellowship, but now if he accepted the living of Framlingham he would lose his Fellowship and he would be able to marry her. It would, however, mean leaving Cambridge, where he had been living for close on fifty years. He was given two months by the College to make up his mind in this difficult situation; at the same time the College warned the next senior, William Wyatt, of the vacancy, and that it "expected that he should get into orders". On March 18 May was presented to the living, but the strain of making up his mind on the prospect of leaving Cambridge and of marrying Mary Barker had been too much for him, and three days later he tried to hang himself. Later he resigned the living and Wyatt, of whom it was also said that he had been "deranged in his intellects", went to Framlingham, and was there for many years. May remained a Fellow till his death five years later, but he seems to have ceased to reside in College. By his will he left all his property to Mary Barker. When she died, the College had some difficulty in securing her bequest, because the old lady had

WILLIAM PITT
(Bust by Nollekens)

ROOMS OCCUPIED BY GRAY AND PITT

The first floor rooms on the left of the picture; they were afterwards occupied successively by E. G. Browne and Aubrey Attwater)

been in the habit of continually altering her will and adding codicils, making more and more legacies, some of them to individual Fellows and scholars of the College, till she had unfortunately left more than she possessed. After legal proceedings the College was awarded £500, of which eventually £440 was received.

Another of the bequests of these years has also a curious story. In 1752 there came into residence, as a Fellow-Commoner, one Joseph Girdler. He never became a Fellow, but he remained in residence in the College in the rooms which are now the senior parlour for over fifty years. Curiously, though he lived immediately under Gray, there is no mention of him in Gray's letters. In 1809 he died, "immensley rich", leaving, besides many legacies, the residue and landed estates to a godson, who was no relative. To the College he left £200, to which his heir added £300. A bequest of £200 entitled him to be buried in the chapel, and in the antechapel the stone next to J. B. is marked Josephus Girdler, A.M.

An infinitely greater benefaction was that of Mrs Sara Lonsdale of Barham Hall. She had been the wife, first of Robert Millicent of Barham, and then of Christopher Lonsdale, a former Tutor of Peterhouse. In honour of William Pitt she decided to leave to Pembroke her estate at Barham, and in anticipation of this bequest Pitt obtained for the College the necessary licence in mortmain to enable the College to receive it. She died in 1807, and by her will directed that one-third of the revenues of the estate should be devoted to the building fund, and also that Barham Hall should be reserved as a private residence for the Master. Unfortunately Joseph Turner, who had in 1790 been appointed to the deanery of Norwich and had to reside there for three to four months in the year, had no use for a third residence and as the will was interpreted by lawyers to prevent him from letting it to anyone, and he would not consent to the College letting it, the house being unoccupied fell into decay.

Turner's absences at Norwich, his great age and perhaps this difference of opinion between him and the Fellows may have adversely affected the College during the last years of his long Mastership. He died on August 3, 1828, aged eighty-three, and the College possesses a remarkable portrait of him, painted by George Dawe and presented by his son.

During the forty-four years of his Mastership over five

hundred and fifty men passed through the College. The Fellow-Commoners became rarer: Archibald John Primrose, afterwards fourth Earl of Rosebery, was among the last of this type. Senior men, however, especially doctors of medicine, continued to join the College, as John Haslam, a writer on insanity, Benjamin Guy Babington, who, invalided from civil service in India, became a distinguished physician at Guy's Hospital, and James Alderson, President of the College of Physicians. The attraction of the Moses exhibitions now reinforced by the connection between College and school in the headmastership of A. W. Trollope drew from Christ's Hospital to Pembroke a number of the ablest scholars of a notable period in the school's history, as Thomas Mitchell, the classical scholar and Fellow of Sidney Sussex, John Greenwood, first a Fellow of Peterhouse and then Trollope's successor as Headmaster of his old school, and Thomas Barnes, the powerful Editor of *The Times*. A number of the scholars of this period obtained Fellowships at other Colleges, as Temple Chevallier, Tutor of St Catharine's, and William French, Master of Jesus. Among the many members of Turner's own family who came to Pembroke, George James Turner became a Lord Justice of Appeal, and Dawson Turner was well known as a banker, botanist and antiquary. Other antiquaries were D. E. Davy, A. I. Suckling, the historian of Suffolk, and Edward Miller, the organist and historian of Doncaster, who took his degree of Mus.Doc. from Pembroke. Popular drama was represented by E. J. Eyre, and John Soane, the son of the architect. Among others distinguished for scholarship were H. S. Boyer, whose academic career ended abruptly, but who afterwards taught Mrs Browning Greek, and Lancelot Sharp, who after producing while an undergraduate an edition of Chatterton's poems became a master at Merchant Taylors' School.

In 1836, the year in which B. E. Sparke, Bishop of Ely, died and Edward Maltby was promoted from Chichester to Durham, W. G. Broughton was appointed Bishop of Sydney, so that Turner's Mastership had produced the first bishop in India and the first bishop in Australia.

CHAPTER VI

THE MODERN COLLEGE

Fourteen years before Joseph Turner's death Gilbert Ainslie had been elected into a Fellowship. He was the son of Henry Ainslie, the former Fellow. In 1816 while still a Bachelor of Arts he became one of the Tutors with William French, and when French was in 1820 elected Master of Jesus, Ainslie became Senior Tutor, first with John Phear, afterwards Rector of Earl Stonham from 1824 to 1881, and then with Henry Tasker, afterwards Vicar of Soham from 1832 to 1874 and a Benefactor of the College. In 1821 he was Senior Treasurer, and in the following year he persuaded the College to buy in certain leases of parts of Paschal Close, the property belonging to Corpus Christi College which lay between the Fellows' large garden and Pembroke Street. Ainslie himself has written the account of these negotiations.

Soon after my election into the office of College Treasurer, having learned that Thomas Mortlock Esq.... had just obtained from Christi College a renewal of a lease of another part of this property for 40 years from Midsummer, 1822, for the express purpose of letting it on a building lease, I represented to the College the expediency of purchasing the Lease for themselves: not merely on account of the nuisance which a row of Houses overlooking the College Orchard would be, but because if ever the College itself should be rebuilt, an *increase* of its site would be highly desirable and *that* it would be difficult, if not impossible ever to obtain, if this ground were ever once occupied by Houses.

The lease was purchased, and as the College already held a lease of the rest of the Close, negotiations were opened with Corpus for the purchase of the fee-simple, but on part of the site being valued the price proved "too startling for any of us and it was needless to value the rest".

The great improvement recently made in the Town as well as the vast influx of young men to the University on the conclusion of the war was the cause of this incredible increase in the value of building ground.

Ainslie, however, in spite of the deterrent price kept the matter open with Corpus for the next six years, and on his election to the Mastership persuaded the Fellows to support him in a definite offer. Negotiations were protracted, but Corpus, "being one and all desirous of doing a neighbourly act", finally offered to exchange the site for ten thousand pounds, invested in land, and this offer was accepted by Pembroke on May 31, 1831. Pembroke had just sold under compulsion the property in London which had been given to the College in the fifteenth century by Sir Philip Bothe and which was now required for widening the approaches to London Bridge, and this sale enabled the College to buy for exchange with Corpus a property at Norwood, near March in the Isle of Ely, and on June 10, 1833, the exchange was effected by means of an Act of Parliament, and Paschal Close, on which now stand Pitt Buildings, the Old Master's Lodge and New Court, was added to the College site. Throughout his Mastership Ainslie continued this policy of increasing the site of the College. When the Leys had been enclosed, Peterhouse had acquired most of that part called Swinecroft to the south of the College orchard, so that extension in that direction seemed stopped. In 1850 however the College bought through Ainslie a property, known as Nelson's Court, on Trumpington Street to the south of the Lodge of the Master of Peterhouse, and five years later exchanged it with Peterhouse for a strip of the enclosed common, and in 1861 a further strip was purchased, together with an observatory which stood on it, and the instruments with which the observatory was equipped. These two strips increased the Fellows' garden so much that they gave up the small garden south of Ivy Court to the Master.

In many other ways during the early years of his Mastership Ainslie showed his power of vigorous action. He was active in preparing the case of the College against the Charity Commissioners concerning the benefaction of Archbishop Grindal, a long litigation which ended in 1830 with the judgment of the Lord Chancellor on appeal that the long lease of Palmersfields formed part of the general property of the College. In 1831 he reorganised the finance of the College, and substituted a more modern system of keeping the accounts for that instituted by William Sampson. In 1842 he started with a personal gift of £200 a fund for the augmentation of the poorer livings of the College.

When he succeeded Turner as Master, he was thirty-five years old, and when five years later, James Wood, the senior Fellow, died, he found himself head of a society every member of which had been his own pupil. Absorbed in the history and traditions of the College he set about the study and preservation of the muniments in the College treasury, and between 1833 and 1847 he compiled a number of manuscript records of very great value. He first transcribed the various codes of statutes by which the College had been governed. In 1835 he completed an account of the site, and his *Annals* of the College. From 1843 to 1846 he was writing out with his own hand an exhaustive calendar of College deeds. In 1847 he completed his *Life* of the Foundress. So much has been done of late years to facilitate the work of students of ancient records, that it is hard to realise the full significance and value of Ainslie's work, but the labour which he put into it must have been prodigious. Matthew Wren had used as the signature of some of his antiquarian collections the words "Moriens ViVam" to indicate his initials; Ainslie at the end of each of his compilations puts the date of completion, and "Gratias Ago".

The inspiration of much of this work upon the records was undoubtedly the approach of the five hundredth anniversary of the Foundation of the College. Ainslie's researches had enabled him to correct the accepted date from 1343 to 1347, and in 1847 the Jubilee was celebrated. January 1st was the statutory date of the Foundress's Feast, and this falling in 1848 on a Sunday, the night of December 31, 1847, was chosen as a suitable occasion for the celebration of the anniversary. As large and distinguished a party was assembled as the smallness of the hall allowed. The inclement season of the year and the prevalence of influenza prevented the attendance of Maltby, then Bishop of Durham, and the only other Pembroke Bishop, Broughton, was in Australia, but George James Turner, Member for Coventry and afterwards Lord Justice of Appeal, and James Alderson, afterwards President of the College of Physicians, represented the Law and Medicine. Most of the reported speeches laid emphasis on the memory of Bishop Ridley:

"This Hall, these Courts, these gardens," said the Vice-Chancellor, "are redolent of his sacred presence." It was to be the last notable party which the College hall, built by the Foundress, was to witness.

Like Matthew Wren Ainslie was an antiquary not merely for the love of antiquity; almost all his collections had a practical bearing on the future of the College, for he combined with a love of tradition a keen desire for reform and progress. At the beginning of an account of all the scholarships founded in the College, to which in 1831 he had persuaded the College to restore the ancient titles, he wrote:

Members of Corporations would do well to reflect that, when sowing a forgetfulness of former benefactions, they are not preparing for themselves a harvest of future liberality. Some persons indeed may be of opinion that the only benefits to be derived from Scholarships are the aid which they afford to the needy, and the encouragement which they extend to the industrious. Undoubtedly these are substantial benefits, and those which were mainly in the contemplation of the Founders. But in most cases the Founders specially enjoined that their own Scholars should be called after their names: and, while this indicated a desire far from blameable, of perpetuating their own memory, so it is not without its proper use. For Antiquity is venerable in the eyes of Youth.

At the time when he became Master there was much talk of reform in Cambridge, and the academic conscience was being stirred somewhat by the knowledge that the existence of ancient statutes which could not in modern conditions be obeyed and the obligation of taking oaths which could not be fulfilled were not calculated to increase and foster a scrupulous attitude throughout the University towards what should be its aims and duties. In the eighteenth century when Roger Long made use of his power of veto to delay the election of Gray's friends, Tuthill and Mason, to Fellowships at Pembroke, Gray had complained of the inability of lawyers "to interpret into Common-Sense Statutes made by old Monks, or Monk-directed old Women", and during the ninety or more years which had passed since that complaint certain parts of the College statutes had become even more impracticable.

Ainslie's careful study of them enabled him to draft a revised code, which was submitted in 1837 to the queen with a petition that it might be enacted. The petition was for seven years in the hands of the Privy Council, and in 1844 the new statutes were granted, "a careful revision and correction with a view of rendering them more conformable to present practice and better adapted to modern conditions, yet without losing sight of the will and intention of the Foundress". The alterations were chiefly concerned with those provisions of the Elizabethan code, which the change in the value of money or in the methods of teaching in the University had made obsolete. For instance, under the old code a private income of ten marks (£6. 13s. 4d.) disqualified a man from a Fellowship. This proviso cannot have been obeyed for many years —Samuel May for instance received more than that as interest on money which he lent to the College—and Ainslie's code substituted for ten marks the average value of a double Fellowship. The commons allowance of eighteenpence a week for each Fellow was altered to a moderate allowance to be fixed from time to time by the College. The customary payment of an annual dividend, computed from the income received in the previous year, was now given the statutory sanction which it had hitherto lacked, but at the same time contribution to a fund for repairs to College buildings was made a prior charge upon the divisible revenues. The old disputations in Chapel, long abandoned, although each Fellow on election had to swear that he would take his part in them, were abolished, and for the long and complicated election oath a simple one of adherence to the Christian religion was substituted. The ancient injunctions to dine in Hall "modeste et sine murmure" and to use no language except Latin disappear. Ainslie's own researches are reflected in the restoration of the ancient name of "Collegium de Valence Marie" for the incorrect Elizabethan "Collegium Mariae Valentiae", and all the old forms of election, the obligation on a certain number of the Fellows to take Holy Orders, and the old statutory date for elections on the tenth of October remained unaltered.

In altering the election oaths Ainslie was following up a policy which he had already been pressing upon the University. In 1833 he published a "most accurate and learned historical analysis" of

the oaths exacted by the University, and had proposed the sub-
stitution of an affirmation for oath to be taken on matriculation
and on taking the B.A. degree, of which his friend the reforming
Dean of Ely, George Peacock, wrote that it "will be remembered
as not one of the least of his many claims upon the gratitude of the
University, for his able and vigilant administration of its affairs
during the two years that he filled the office of vice-chancellor".
Ainslie had been Vice-Chancellor in the first year of his Mastership
and again in 1836. During his second tour of office he laid the
foundation stones both of Cockerell's Building in the University
Library and of the Fitzwilliam Museum. Though ardent for reform
he held that it should come from inside the University. This was
not however the view of many, who despaired of anything really
valuable being done without external compulsion and direction.
Agitation for a Royal Commission was being carried on and the
Government yielded to the demand. Ainslie persuaded the University to appoint a syndicate to advise upon the revision of the
statutes, but the Commission reported in 1852, and among other
recommendations was one for the abolition of Fellowships and
Scholarships tied to schools or localities. Ainslie at once opened
negotiations with Christ's Hospital, Merchant Taylors' School,
and the Borough of Ipswich for an agreed division of the endowments which should free the Moses, Parkin, Stuart, Smart and
Scrivener Scholarships from such restrictions. But when the
Government took the further step of appointing a Commission
to make new statutes for the University and for the Colleges,
Ainslie felt that a principle was at stake, which not even his genuine
desire for reform could sacrifice. In order that the College might
be free from the condition of Grindal's benefaction to elect scholars
and Fellows from St Bee's School or from the counties of Cumberland and Westmorland, it was necessary to obtain Parliamentary
sanction, and Ainslie arranged that the Act of Parliament appointing the Statutory Commissioners should have a special clause
for this purpose. To get this clause correctly worded he worked
unceasingly, writing direct to the Lord Chancellor and to the
Minister in charge of the Bill in the House of Commons, and having
occasion to point out an error in the body of the Bill, he noted
down at the end of the copy of his letter: "My sole reason for

pointing out the error in the bill adverted to above was to con-
ciliate...favour towards my own College. The Bill itself I looked
upon as an abomination." So, too, in the Latin autobiography
which he wrote in the register of Fellows, when he mentions the
new statutes made by the Commissioners for the College, he
records that he took no part in the framing of them, because he
held that no one had a right to change the statutes and ordinances
of the Foundress, unless they were clearly meaningless and
damaging [nisi plane inepta sint aut damnosa], and having recorded
this he closes his autobiography sadly with a prayer for the future
of the College, "Ut Collegium sub novis regulis valeat tristis
Deum precatur". The changes, too, in the statutes of the University, although many of them had been recommended by the
Syndicate of which he had been a member, were not all such that
he could accept them. The chief controversy in the University
had been about the power to be allowed in future to the Heads of
Houses. The Syndicate had left a great measure of control in their
hands, but this was not really acceptable to the majority of resi-
dents, and on this point Ainslie had against him several Fellows of
his own College—Arlett, Adams, Haig Brown and Ferguson.
"Academicis non placuit", he wrote in the autobiography, "ut
Magistri Collegiorum aliquam in Universitate haberent potes-
tatem", and he added that from that date he decided that the
management of University affairs ought to be left to those who
had sought the power. He adds that he had played his part in
settling the long quarrels between the University and the Town
and that he rejoiced most of all that his last work had been a work
of peace.

Consequently, the last years of his Mastership were years of
solitary detachment from the life of the College which he had
served so nobly. In 1862 the College decided to repair the organ
in the chapel, which had fallen into disrepair through lack of use
in the eighteenth century, but since the Master disliked the playing
of organs, it was rarely played except when he was absent from
the lodge. To undergraduates he rarely spoke; on one occasion,
when one of them had received news of the serious illness of a
parent and could not find the Tutor for leave to go home, he dared
to wait upon the Master, and at dinner in hall that day his boldness

was commented on almost in a whisper, but on his return to College he reported the Master as having been very kind. Nevertheless here lay the weakness of Ainslie's Mastership, since in numbers and in the standard of scholarship the College sank in the middle of the century to a state which can only be compared with the lean years of which Gray complained in the eighteenth century. For the first fourteen years that Ainslie was Master the average of admissions kept up to about fifteen, and these years produced Sir George Stokes, Sir Henry Maine, and J. R. Woodford, Bishop of Ely. Others too made their mark in later life, G. E. Day who was professor of Medicine at St Andrews, and two brothers, Edward and Peter Frederick Shortland, the elder of whom was a great worker among the Maoris and the younger the only admiral whom the College has hitherto bred.

During the next sixteen years, while Ainslie was busiest with College business and University reform, the average entry sank to less than nine a year. To 1841 and 1842 belong William Haig Brown, Master of Charterhouse School, of which he was "second Founder", J. B. Phear, son of the former Tutor and afterwards a Fellow of Clare and Chief Justice of Ceylon, and Timothy Holmes, who became a distinguished surgeon. Both Haig Brown and Holmes were later to be Honorary Fellows of the College, and in 1847, the Jubilee year, there came into residence Charles Edward Searle. But otherwise the academic record of these sixteen years is poor indeed, and though something must be allowed for disappointed ambitions the account of the College at this time written by D'Arcy Wentworth Thompson shows some of the cause. Thompson had been at Christ's Hospital and went first to Trinity, but attracted by the greater emoluments of the close scholarships he migrated to Pembroke in 1848. In 1868 he published his *Wayside Thoughts* in which he gave an account of his life at Cambridge. He admitted later that when he wrote these sketches he was "full of reforming notions, convinced of my own infallibility, and inclined to reach out irreverent hands to steady ancient and Sacred Arks", but even so the picture which he drew of Pembroke in the middle of the nineteenth century, though exaggerated, must be faced. Veiling the College under the name of St Ignavia's he wrote: "Nowhere in the world, save, perhaps, in the heart of China, would you light upon so delightful, peaceful, drowsy, comfortable, venerable, useless a caravanserai of idleness. Such institutions in our midst are relics of a dead and gone civilisation. They moulder away in a beautiful and ivy-clad decay, and putrefy with a not unpleasing odour, like the odour of church-incense." He describes the elementary and unsatisfying lectures given in College, the mathematical lectures in a garret in Ivy Court. "The ceiling sloped very uncomfortably down to the ground, some panes in the window were broken, and a dismal fire gave out a little surly warmth reluctantly." Of the Fellows, about ten were resident, and these "were for the most part of the cobra kind. They had swallowed their intellectual goat in early life, and were passing through the years of inactivity requisite for diges-tion".[1] Of his fellow-undergraduates he wrote: "A few were youths of pleasant, gentlemanly ways; some able and unambitious; others—the majority—of moderate abilities and slender attain-ments; the greater portion were in the possession of independent means, seeking the easiest possible road to genteel dilettante ecclesiasticism; a small minority were illiterate beyond all re-demption, but, at the same time, were hearty, likable, hospitable fellows." Thompson's own chance of a Fellowship—he was a Browne medallist in 1849 and bracketed sixth Classic in 1852—may have been a little prejudiced in March 1851, when he was admonished for "riotous behaviour at Huntingdon", but by the time he was eligible the vacancy had been filled. After some years as a schoolmaster at Edinburgh Academy he became Professor of Greek at Queen's College, Galway. The man whose election had closed the door to his preferment in Pembroke was Searle, and the next vacancy in 1853 was filled by John Couch Adams, the brilliant young mathematician from St John's, who had dis-covered the planet Neptune. Yet though disappointment and youthful infallibility may have coloured Thompson's picture of St Ignavia there must have been some truth in it, for the following facts speak for themselves. In 1858 one man was admitted to the College in March; he came up as a freshman in October, and the following note in the Terms Book describes his career: "Came

---

[1] That this was exaggeration can be seen from the fact that among the resident Fellows were Stokes, Haig Brown, Power, and Beatson.

Oct. 18. Left College and went to Caius after keeping five days Oct. 22."

At the beginning of the previous year John Power had been left as sole Tutor, Haig Brown having married and left the College for the headmastership of a school at Kensington. The experience of 1858 must have been a little discouraging to Power, but during the years which followed things began to look somewhat better. For the last twelve years of Ainslie's Mastership the average entry rose to twelve, and was not altogether undistinguished. A. W. Sillitoe, the first President of the P.C.D.S., which was founded in 1862, became Bishop of New Westminster, and E. Bickersteth was largely responsible for the foundation of the Cambridge Mission to Delhi and was later Bishop of Central Japan. T. C. Fry was Headmaster of Berkhampstead and a very active Dean of Lincoln. G. F. Warner was Keeper of Manuscripts at the British Museum and an Honorary Fellow of the College. J. A. Paton and W. A. Prince were Benefactors of the College. J. C. Rust, Vicar of Soham, was probably the only man who preached a sermon in Esperanto in the University Church. J. B. Wilson was the first Pembroke Rowing Blue and E. J. Heriz-Smith, one of the great "characters" of nineteenth-century Pembroke, was the subject of a *Vanity Fair* cartoon.

Gilbert Ainslie died on January 9, 1870. Five days later the Fellows, under the Presidency of Benjamin Wrigglesworth Beatson, who had held his Fellowship since 1827, unanimously appointed John Power to the Mastership. Power with shrewd judgment brought back Searle from the care of a Suffolk living to be Tutor and it is from 1870 that the modern history of Pembroke may well be dated. In the first place, this year saw the beginning of an ambitious and drastic building scheme, inspired in part by a fear that unused balances in college building funds might be diverted to University purposes. The architect chosen was Alfred Waterhouse and in a preliminary letter he sketched a reconstruction of the whole College. The scheme included a new chapel with a campanile, though the architect recognised that the removal of Sir Christopher Wren's work would be a matter of regret. The College decided first to proceed with a range of new buildings (Red Buildings) south of the chapel and with a new Master's

GILBERT SCOTT'S ADDITION TO THE CHAPEL

THE COLLEGE FROM THE AIR

lodge to the east of Ivy Court. When this work was completed in 1873 and the old Master's lodge was vacated, the problem of the Old Court became urgent. The architect's view was definite: while he was aware that a strong feeling existed in favour of retaining the court in its original dimensions he nevertheless preferred a "more spacious and airy courtyard". The College followed this lead and authorised the demolition of the old lodge and the south side of the court with a view to the enlargement of the hall. At this point there was no intention to pull down the hall. But the fatal step had been taken. With the old lodge gone, the hall "wore a singularly forlorn and desolate aspect" and on March 16, 1875, the following laconic entry appears in the College Order Book: "It was agreed that Mr Waterhouse be authorised to pull down the College Hall." In spite of protests from old Pembroke men and a spirited correspondence in *The Times* the order was carried out. The new hall was begun in 1875 and shortly afterwards the College approved the same architect's plans for a new library and lecture-rooms. Thus, in the short space of five years was the College enlarged and rebuilt. There were plans, too, for a drastic treatment of the chapel and the old library; but the passion for destruction cooled. George Gilbert Scott (son of Sir Gilbert and father of Sir Giles) was consulted and gave his opinion that to sacrifice the old library would be a mistake; for the chapel he proposed an extension at the east end with an arch between the original body of the chapel and the extension. After skilful postponement of the Waterhouse proposals, these suggestions were eventually adopted, together with the plans for a new building on the corner of Pembroke Street and Tennis Court Road. This building, originally known as Lodge Court and afterwards as New Court, was completed in 1882.

The primary motive for this addition to the College fabric was, of course, the increase in the number of undergraduates. When Power became Master in 1870, there were 43 undergraduates on the boards; when Searle succeeded to the Mastership in 1880, there were 122—and the growth continued. In this period the College received a notable bequest under the will of B. W. Beatson, who left the sum of £10,000 to the College, as well as about 5000 books to the library. Part of the money was applied to the foundation of scholarships bearing Mr Beatson's name.

In 1872 a Royal Commission had been appointed and new statutes for the University and the colleges came into force in 1882. The most important changes affected the tenure of Fellowships. Fellows were henceforth allowed to marry without vacating their Fellowships; and Fellowships, which previously could be held for life without residence, were now tenable (after the first six years) only if held with certain College or University offices.

Charles Edward Searle had been Tutor of the College since 1870 and, when he became Master in 1880, he continued to hold the office of Tutor for another ten years. To him, more than to any other single man, the growth of the College, both in numbers and in distinction, during the later part of the nineteenth century, was due. Amongst the senior Fellows who signed the order for his election were Stokes and Adams; amongst the juniors were J. N. Keynes and R. A. Neil. A few years senior to these last was Charles Herman Prior, who had taken his degree from Caius as fourth Wrangler in 1873 and had been elected to a Fellowship at Pembroke in the same year. Robert Alexander Neil, second Classic in 1876, came to a Pembroke Fellowship from Peterhouse and it was Prior and Neil who were Searle's lieutenants in the fashioning of the new Pembroke. Prior became Tutor in 1890 and held the office till his death in 1899; he was succeeded by Neil, who died prematurely less than two years later. So it happened that Searle outlived the two younger men who had helped him most in the government of the College. On Searle's death in 1902 Sir George Gabriel Stokes, who had entered the College in the year of Queen Victoria's accession, was elected in his stead. The new Master was full of years and academical honours. Three years earlier his jubilee as Lucasian Professor of Mathematics had been celebrated in the College by a distinguished gathering of men of science from all over the world. He held the office of Master for less than six months and his successor was Arthur James Mason, of Trinity, Canon of Canterbury and Lady Margaret's Professor of Divinity. Mason was Vice-Chancellor in 1909 and presided over the University, as over the College, with great charm and dignity. It was during his Mastership that Pitt Buildings were built and the erection of the bridge in front of what was then the Master's lodge was due to his munificence. Mason was succeeded, on his retirement to Canterbury in 1912, by William Sheldon Hadley, who had been Tutor for the previous ten years. In 1925 important alterations were made in the hall, which was lengthened by the inclusion of the old combination room. At the same time the Gothic roof was removed and two floors, providing fourteen sets of rooms, were built above the hall. The plaster of the new ceiling was adorned with the arms of the Foundress and of the principal Benefactors of the College. After more than forty years of work devoted to the College, Hadley died suddenly on Christmas Day 1927 and was succeeded by the present Master, Arthur Hutchinson, who had been elected a Fellow in 1892 and had lately become Professor of Mineralogy in the University. More rooms for undergraduates were still an urgent need and in 1930 the College decided to convert the Master's lodge of 1873 into sets of rooms and a new lodge was built from the designs of M. E. Webb in the south-east corner of the garden.

Such is a bare recital of those who have held high office in the College and of the new buildings which have been added to the College fabric during the last fifty years. Of the detailed history of the College and of its personnel during that period it is not possible here to give an adequate account. Transformed from a small college into a large one in the later part of the last century, Pembroke has remained amongst the larger colleges and during the last thirty years, except for the war period, the average annual entry has been between 80 and 100. Between 1914 and 1918 many strange sights were seen in the College. At the outbreak of war it was in Pembroke that the first officers' training school in the country was established. Originally known as "Comber's Irregulars", the school afterwards received full recognition from the War Office. Later, the College became the headquarters of an Officers' Cadet Battalion. The old library was an orderly room; the younger Fellows joined the fighting forces, one (A. A. Seaton) being killed in action; the seniors did war work in Government offices or elsewhere. In 1919 the College was quickly filled again, but the war had taken a heavy toll: on stone tablets in the cloister there are carved the names of three hundred Pembroke men who did not return. The normal life of the College was, however, quickly restored and was livened for a time by the presence of a number of naval officers, who were drafted to Cambridge for a course of six months' work. Like all other colleges, Pembroke was in 1925 given new statutes as prepared by the University Commissioners. The principal changes brought about by these statutes are age-limits for the tenure of college offices, the reservation of a certain proportion of Fellowships for the holders of University teaching offices, and the requirement that no one shall be admitted to residence in a college, unless he has already qualified for matriculation.

In the last ten years death has laid an exceptionally heavy hand upon the Fellows of Pembroke. Edward Granville Browne, one of the greatest orientalists of his time, died in 1926; less than two years later came Hadley's sudden death, to which reference has already been made; there followed the deaths of George Birtwistle (Senior Wrangler in 1899 and a brilliant mathematical teacher) in 1929 and of Nial Patrick McCleland in 1933; finally, in 1935, the College was shattered by the deaths in quick succession of John Cuthbert Lawson, Aubrey Attwater, and Henry Gordon Comber, affectionately known to many generations of men, inside and outside the College, as "the Old Man". Such men as these are not easily replaced.

Yet the House of Valence Marie goes on. In the years since the war Pembroke has given to the world bishops, judges, governors of provinces, members of parliament, university professors, captains of English cricket and football, and the leader of the last two Everest expeditions; the Pembroke boat went Head of the River for the first time in history in 1923, repeated this success from 1931 to 1934 and won the Grand at Henley in 1935; the College Mission, founded in 1885, continues its good work in Walworth.

In recent years one of the most valuable instruments for securing closer cohesion between the College and its old members has been the Pembroke College Society founded by H. G. Comber in 1920. It was at the instigation of Comber and for members of this Society that Attwater primarily wrote this *Historiola*; it is now offered in affectionate memory of those two most loyal sons of the House of Valence Marie.

INDEX

Lightning Source UK Ltd.
Milton Keynes UK
UKHW011936230619
344923UK00001B/13/P

9 781108 015332